Feeding Lions

Sharing the Conservative Philosophy in a
Politically Hostile World

Paul A. Ibbetson

authorHOUSE®

AuthorHouse™
1663 Liberty Drive, Suite 200
Bloomington, IN 47403
www.authorhouse.com
Phone: 1-800-839-8640

First published by AuthorHouse 1/23/2009

ISBN: 978-1-4389-2008-5 (sc)
ISBN: 978-1-4389-2009-2 (hc)

Library of Congress Control Number: 2008911624

Printed in the United States of America
Bloomington, Indiana

This book is printed on acid-free paper.

Table of Contents

Author's Note: *Throughout this book I have used my own previously published articles. For the purpose of this book, these articles have been re-edited for punctuation, grammar and minor word changes. The articles have not changed in form or content from my original published articles and I made these changes in an effort to make this book a more enjoyable reading experience for my audience. The original articles remain at their cited locations in their original format.*

Acknowledgments

SPECIAL THANKS GO TO MY editor, Janice Stong. Thank you for being so supportive of my creative side, and so patient with my inability to give commas their proper due.

This book is dedicated to the average regular person in America who knows there is a God, loves their family, and has come to the realization that the United States is the greatest country on Earth. It's time to be awakened to the fact that you are a conservative.

Introduction

LIFE IS LIKE A TRIP to the zoo. Did you expect a statement like that? Probably not, but I think in time you will understand my unique perspective on life if you just give it a chance. Think about the zoo for a moment. If you haven't been for a while, and many of us have not, the zoo is a place of tremendous diversity. There's beauty, ugliness, examples of strength, and, unfortunately at times, displays of lethargy and malaise. The zoo has a sense of safety about it but, no matter what precautions are taken, there is also an aura of potential danger. Within the walls and fences that comprise the confines of the zoo, there are creatures that exude a wondrous intelligence while others appear virtually mindless.

Does that sound like real life? Give me time. I suppose any analogy could be used to depict life as well as the focus of this book, politics, but like the jungles in which many of the animals in the zoo are collected, I believe this view of the world will be especially fruitful. I think it is particularly important to say, before we get too far down the road, that this book is a serious endeavor to share the conservative philosophy. This book covers many of the most highly contentious subjects of the day including: political correctness, border security, the Patriot Act, the War on Terror, and global warming, among others. Taking a stand on these issues guarantees an argument and opposition from many sides. As a matter of fact, most people won't step into this cage because of the potential damage that can take place to one's career, family, and friends. In short, spreading the conservative philosophy is a lot like feeding lions, it's not something you take lightly or you're going to get eaten.

Feeding Lions is, in part, a compilation of articles I have written for the 35 news and political websites that have been kind enough to publish my work. These articles are placed within my own unique conservative philosophy of life which includes personal observations and research on individuals across the board, from Michael Savage to Al Gore.

With all that said, I have a powerful weapon in the fight against liberals, humor. I unleash this weapon with reckless disregard and I'm sure from time to time I see, out of the corner of my eye, a few liberals chuckling along, right before they send in their hate mail.

So how's it going so far? Intrigued? Curious? Excited? Or have I made you angry already? All I can say is, give me time.

Chapter 1

Escaping My Cage

IT WOULD SEEM COMPLETELY UNFAIR to share a philosophy on the superior components of conservatism without telling you a little about myself and how I became the person I am today. I was born in Iola, Kansas, on January 9, 1969. Some of my first memories come from Kansas State University where my parents were young struggling students and I, one of two children in tow, learned about liberalism straight from the bowels of academia. Here are a few examples from the old memory banks. I remember stepping over rows of sunbathing co-eds to get into the on-campus family housing. I remember the giant university murals that were coined "modern art." An especially interesting piece that caught my attention was a set of curved images that looked like a set of multi-colored buttocks that, at my tender young age, I succinctly called the "hiney picture." Ah, the '70s. I remember how university liberalism brought a father and son together when I asked my father why a couple walking arm-in-arm down the street both had such beautiful long hair. I remember my father slowing, attempting to walk me through an explanation of the hippie culture, while my wide eyes followed the explanation as best I could at a young age. Of course I think for my father a difficult explanation turned almost impossible when the couple turned to face us. The matching set of beautiful hair was then complimented with a matching set of full mustaches. My follow-up questions began immediately and, for the life of me, I can't remember how my father worked his way through that explanation. I regret losing that memory because I think it would have been classic.

I grew up on a farm in Southeast Kansas where our nearest neighbor was about two miles away. There are several unique things that come from living on a farm. I think the isolation of country living brings about a sense of self sufficiency city folks never contemplate. I also think there is a general misconception about farming. Farming is actually part science, part luck, and a whole heck of a lot of hard work. When I got a little older and really began to listen to my father about farming I was amazed at the complexity of the cycles of crop rotation and the science involved in bringing about a good crop.

My father taught me many lessons and they were all hard fought as I was a stubborn child to say the least. I think the three most important lessons he taught me were: work hard, do a quality job, and finish each project you start. There was a lot of blood, sweat, and tears in these lessons but they have served me well. My mother taught me the verbal skills of communication which have opened many doors where my father's teaching can be implemented. Family was, and remains, an important component of my life. I could not think of life without family and it is an important part of the conservative philosophy.

It was early in my life that I was taught about capitalism by my hardworking uncles in the never ending hay fields of Yates Center, Kansas. I learned the value of money earned and that there was no inherent evil in making a profit for selling something people wanted. Basically, the direct opposite of everything liberals would spew my way later in life. I am ever appreciative to the values I learned in those burning hot hay fields.

Politics were not a focus of life growing up as work took precedence. I remember a general feeling of disheartenment among family and friends during the Jimmy Carter administration. There was a feeling of misery with the Carter administration far before I learned about the misery index. High unemployment and high interest rates were a concern, but it seemed that people felt a loss of something the country previously had that I would only begin to understand when Ronald Reagan became President. I was in high school when Ronald Reagan became President and I would never pretend I was the political animal that I am today. To prove that point, when interviewed by my high school paper concerning my thoughts about Ronald Reagan after the John Hinckley assassination attempt, my response was simply, "Well, he can take a bullet." That quote was repeated for a long time but it reflected my ignorance of politics as much as a tendency toward humor. What I did know about Reagan was that he was tough and unafraid. Even lacking knowledge of politics, I knew and respected courage when I saw it. After Jimmy Carter, Ronald Reagan was a breath of fresh air. I also understood that for some reason liberals really hated him. Later, the Reagan legacy would have a much greater meaning to me and I wish I had focused a little more on what Reagan was fighting for and a little less on where the cheerleaders were going.

I spent the first few years after high school as an academic gypsy, attending three different colleges, without a real understanding of what I wanted to do with my future. I stopped going to college before I graduated and started working in the public sector. After several years of being a restaurant manager, grocery store assistant manager, among others, I started a career in law enforcement almost by chance.

A friend of mine, Mike Doyle, a law enforcement officer himself, encouraged me to apply and, after refusing the job once, I found myself a policeman. When a zoo expands its facilities and animals are placed in larger habitats, I have often pondered how the animals are affected. Do they think, "Wow! This is great! More space to roam" or do they think, "Wonderful, I finally understand my space and now you're changing the rules." It's probably the former because animals have a built-in need to roam and a lack of personal baggage, such as fear of change, which often prevents people from seeking their full potential. I believe many people often keep themselves in their own little familiar cages, as safe, secure, prisoners. Having taken a leap to the most adventurous career of my life was like walking out of a little pen into the great outdoors.

It was not easy, change, that is. I remember being extremely nervous by the scrutiny involved in the law enforcement hiring process. Today, compared to fighting liberals in every state in the union, let alone international moon bats, those early days were extremely scary for a little country boy exchanging name tags and aprons for a badge and gun. Of course, this transition from the sheltered cage of my previous existence had its funny moments. One pre-employment interview took place in the presence of a five-member panel which included the Mayor, Chief of Police, City Attorney, City Administrator, and a member of the Clergy. I was so nervous following the interview that I left the building, drove home, and realized I was sitting behind the wheel of somebody else's car! Yes, it's true. As it happened, the clergy member of the panel had a vehicle of a similar make and model as my own and he had left his keys in the ignition. When I left City Hall my mind was racing through the events of the interview and I never noticed my car was parked a couple spots up the street. It was only in the driveway of my home that I noticed the key ring in the ignition was not my own. I guess you could say that I did my first criminal investigation, in which I found that I was the bad guy. Oh man! I raced back to City Hall wondering how this was going to play out. I was certain that stealing a preacher's car, who was a member of the hiring committee, couldn't be a plus for my chances of employment. I also wondered if I might go from job applicant to convict all in the same day. Talk about getting thrown back in the small cage! I was thinking on those verbal skills my mother taught me when I approached City Hall. I parked in the same parking spot and looked around. Everything appeared normal. No people in search of a villain, no posse on the march. I took the chance that no one knew what had happened, got in my car, and drove home. The next day I was hired. That event, and others to follow, taught me that succeeding in life involves not only hard work and knowing when to take advantage of opportunities, but also a little bit of luck.

My political awakening began as a police officer. In many ways I have come to believe that law enforcement is every bit as much a political position as any elected mayor, councilman, congressman, or even president. As well, small town politics are every bit as perplexing, anxiety provoking, and even dangerous as anything on the national level. After a couple years on the job, I came to realize that life could be as interesting and dangerous as a trip to the zoo. It all depends on which side of the cage you are on. I learned to "feed lions" when I was a police officer for the first time. That is, I had to make big decisions that affected people's lives. These decisions were rarely popular with everyone. This was a turning point in my life when I learned that in the end all you have is your integrity. I found that if you are honest with people they respect you more, no matter what they say to your face, than they do the spineless jellyfish trying to make everyone happy. I also learned a disdain for the political rhinos early on and it remains my belief today.

To my good fortune, I had the opportunity to work with criminal justice thinkers like Doug Murphy who taught me that the passion to help people could be enhanced by thoughtful strategy and, even more importantly, that if I was brave enough to take a stand, I could at least change my little part of the world. In the zoo of life, Murphy was a true frontiersman, a cage breaker if you will, and under his tutelage I joined the dangerous and adventurous work in the Montgomery County Drug Task Force. I began to learn that the sky was the limit to what I could achieve. Later, after climbing the ladder to the level of Chief of Police, the pinnacle of a political position that was never meant to be a political position, I toed the line of political correctness and followed the good old boy practice of backroom back scratching that secured my career success until retirement. Uh, not quite. Instead, I charged the mayor and several members of the city government with corruption violations which led to the first successful recall election in Montgomery County history. Those were stressful times and a true test of my will to do the right thing. I learned, without question, that if you want to make people mad, tell the truth and do the right thing; works every time.

After winning the battle with city corruption, I made another major life decision. This decision was whether to settle in a law enforcement career for life, or attempt something new. For me, along with so many other Americans, September 11, 2001, had a profound effect on how I looked at life. After looking at the death and destruction of that day, I began to see the fencing of my own life start to close in again and it was soon time to break loose into a new career which would allow me to have a stronger effect on the world.

By 2002, I found myself back in academia finishing my Bachelors' degree that had been changed for the umpteenth time to criminal justice, which felt right for what I believed was my calling to deal with national security. I later found that this important subject could only be dealt with by addressing the politics behind the actions and inactions of the government to protect this country. After packing my bags and escaping my own cage of safe familiarity and inability to relocate away from family and friends, I was surprised to see just how liberal university life had become in the 12 years I had been away from those hallowed halls. Had things changed so much or had I just been oblivious to what was being spoon fed to me in the past? Now don't get me wrong, I've had many good professors and still do; however, it is impossible to deny the liberal flavor that resides within the university world.

I earned my Bachelor's degree and a Master's degree in criminal justice from Wichita State University. Today, I find myself still entrenched within the classroom, working my way through a challenging doctorate program at Kansas State University. Yes, I'm walking those same streets I walked as a child with my parents when they expanded their horizons and, surely, it must be a small world.

There is no doubt that you now know all you ever wanted to know about me, and possibly much more, but there is a reason behind this disclosure. Think about how many times you have watched the drive-by media disparage some individual or organization without any context or accountability. How many times have you heard a politician avoid giving their past history or just avoid disclosure in general? It happens all the time and it's cowardly, but not in this book. In these pages you will know me, where I'm coming from, and where we can go forward together if you so desire. Honesty, it's my strategy; now let's go to the zoo.

Chapter 2

If It Smells, Clean It

IF IT SMELLS, CLEAN IT. This is not a profound statement, it's simple common sense. Any zoo keeper can tell you it's a part of the daily routine to expel the growing excrement before it contaminates all the animals who call the zoo their home. This is a problem in real life as well. Today we have many contaminants that threaten to soil our traditional values and create a new country far different from the intentions of our founding fathers. The painful truth is that the battle to maintain a free America based on our traditional Judeo-Christian values within a capitalistic free market system is a battle being waged by agents within this country. It is the far left radicals we often term "liberals" who wage this battle, and their arsenal includes the television media, newspapers, and magazines, just to name a few. However, I believe that one of the most potent weapons of the left is not a component of the information industry, but the pervasive ideology of political correctness. Liberals will tell you that political correctness is a myth, an urban legend created by conservatives to have justification to judge and attack innocent people. Think about that for a moment and you will begin to understand how interesting a tool of ideological warfare political correctness has become.

First, political correctness ties into the philosophy of moral relativism where right and wrong is simply a point of perception from the individual's standpoint. Simply put, if you don't believe it's wrong then it's not wrong. It's an extremely convenient philosophy that allows the practitioner to completely bypass biblical scripture as the moral template and to replace it with human judgment. I have aptly called political correctness the mental neutering of this country because, as the movement progresses, intelligent traditional free thinking people become beaten down to a point where they can no longer separate right from wrong and, when the evils of political correctness are so glaring that they cannot be avoided, these same people then lack the fortitude to address the obvious problem. The teeth within the political correctness strategy is not only to numb the mind to right and wrong with moral relativism, but to viciously attack those who would debate right and wrong on issues as intolerant haters. To validate my assertions on political correctness one has only to think back to the last time they heard a lecture or discussion on a political or social issue that was so far off base that they wanted to scream in opposition but, strangely enough, remained silent because to give verbal opposition on the issue just would not seem as "proper" or be accepted by somebody somewhere. If you are honest with yourself, you will have to admit that this probably happens to you almost every day. The victims of political correctness are not simply numbers on a chart, they are you and me. Inevitably, it will be the entire nation. I choose to fight this scourge whenever I encounter it. For your own reflection, I wish to forward one of my articles on this important subject that addresses political correctness as it has been applied to squelching not only judgments made about radical Islam, but the inclusion of any kind of debate concerning the lack of public rejection of terrorism by the domestic U.S. Muslim population.

Death of a Messenger

Don't kill the messenger! You've heard that saying before and it has as much relevance today as in the past. Ages ago, before the wondrous technologies for long distance communication were available, the means of sending messages between individuals over great distances fell to the responsibility of the humble messenger. The messenger, whether on foot or horseback, would battle assorted dangers, be it inclement weather, sickness, wolves, or rogue bandits to see his message delivered safely to its recipient. Unfortunately, surviving the successful delivery of a message was often not the hardest part of the job. You see, sometimes people would become angry with a message that they did not wish to receive and the messenger became an easy outlet for this misguided anger.

Recently, I was an observer of a death of sorts of a fellow carrier of the conservative message of truth. A fellow radio associate and conservative columnist, Chuck Armstrong, found himself at the end of the proverbial sword from his college newspaper publisher when his weekly opinion column contained comments about the violent aspects of the religion of Islam. Armstrong penned the column after researching the topic which included personal communications from well known scholar Robert Spencer. Not only was Armstrong's column rejected but insinuations of racism were put forward. When Armstrong questioned the validity of rejecting an opinion piece on this topic, he was fired as a contributing columnist for the college newspaper.

Now you may be thinking that Chuck Armstrong was attending a liberal college where the conservative ideas and opinions are squelched as a matter of college policy, maybe at Berkley or the liberal breeding grounds of Columbia University, right? If you thought that was the case you would be way off. Would you be surprised if I said it was at Kansas State University? Yes, that's right, here in the heartland, the Bible belt, the place I like to call common sense central from the growing scourge of liberalism. Yes, even here, to bring forth a message that asks people to think hard about a religion so relevant to current events in the nation doesn't get you a debate, it gets you fired. I would leave it in the capable hands of the American people to read Armstrong's article and make up their own minds if his message pains them because it's off base, or if it only hurts because it's painfully accurate?

Unfortunately, I believe that Armstrong was forced to taste the steel of the Kansas State University Collegian because he violated the laws of political correctness. Yes, political correctness, the mental neutering of this country that not only day by day clouds the division between right and wrong, but breaks the will to question anything for fear that some group or organization may be offended. Most often these groups are liberals. Options were all this college newspaper had in this case. They could have collected an opposing opinion piece to Armstrong's and ran them on the same page. They could have printed any disclaimer of their choosing before the article. Now here is a novel idea, they could have ran the article and let the readers decide and hold the author accountable through the usage of letters to the editor which the newspaper has every week. In the end, the Kansas State University Collegian decided to pass on all these options and to liquidate Armstrong for delivering a message that does not meet the liberal standard of political correctness. That message has been heard loud and clear. (Ibbetson, 2007, October 15)

I would like to thank Chuck Armstrong for allowing me to use his article in this book. In doing so, he again steps into the lion's den of scrutiny and I gladly stand beside him at feeding time. Because of Armstrong's willingness to share his article in this book, readers can now see the debate he was attempting to create and make their own judgments about its validity.

Religion of Violence
by Chuck Armstrong
Liberals act dangerously to compare Islam to Christianity

'Radical Christianity is just as threatening as radical Islam, in a country like America,' Rosie O'Donnell told millions of Americans when she was still a host on "The View." This skewed attitude is not unique to O'Donnell; it is one shared by many liberals across the country. Too many individuals are scared to admit the truth, that Islam is nothing like Christianity or any other religion based on Judeo-Christian principles. It is, in fact, a religion of violence.

In a span of four debates, not one Democratic presidential candidate said the words "Islamic terrorists." Instead, the candidates – and many other liberals – each tiptoe around the idea that a religion is the foundation of terrorism. However, when the facts are examined, it is hard to deny that Islam is a violent religion, and one that has bred terrorism.

The Koran contains many verses that are violent. Now, this is not to dismiss the fact that there are also violent verses in the Bible, the book that many Christians hold to be the Word of God. The difference, however, is that the verses in the Bible are merely descriptive; the verses found in the Koran are prescriptive. 'In the Koran, there are open ended universal commands for believers to wage war against non-believers,' says Robert Spencer, author of numerous books that examine the history and theology of Islam. 'There is nothing that is like that in the Bible anywhere.' In chapter nine verse 29 of the Koran, believers are called to 'fight against those who…do not truly believe either in God or the Last Day…till they [have been] humbled in war.'

Verses in the Koran are not the only source of violence found in Islam. The belief of jihad is also a violent concept that many Islamists carry out. This is not to say that every Muslim practices jihad or is a violent individual, but Islam as a whole is a system that calls its believers to practice this "holy war."

Another belief that many liberals, including O'Donnell, share is that this country's occupation of Iraq has created terrorists and violence. This could not be farther from the truth. In 1998, Osama bin Laden wrote an article with a few other radical jihadists that called for a fatwa, or a legal ruling, to all Muslims to kill Americans and their allies. In the article, bin Laden says, 'The ruling to kill the Americans and their allies – civilians and military – is an individual duty for every Muslim who can do it…' The article goes on to say, 'This is in accordance with the words of Almighty Allah…' First off, this article goes on to promote the idea that Islam is a religion of violence. However, it also makes aware the notion that jihadists wanted Americans dead long before Operation Iraqi Freedom. In fact, this article was written three years before the horrific attacks on September 11th, 2001.

Americans need to stand up for Western civilization and Judeo-Christian principles, the same principles that this country was founded on. 'Whether or not we are

Christians ourselves...the Judeo-Christian civilization is still something we are enjoying the benefits of living in the Western world,' Spencer says. 'To attack Christianity, ultimately, is to attack one of the foundations of this civilization.'

The religion of Islam promotes the destruction of every foundation of America. Even though not every Islamist believes this is right, the basis of this religion is to destroy any and all non-believers. To side with Islam is to side with the enemy of America.

Political correctness is, without a doubt, a powerful tool of the left to squash debate; however, they don't apply it to everyone. Whether it is Ward Churchill, Rosie O'Donnell, or many other repugnant orators of anti-American propaganda, liberals for the most part remain silent until conservatives are behind the microphone.

I spoke about the far left having control of the media machine in general. This observation is absolutely true save for one media outlet – talk radio. When it comes to talk radio, conservatives own the airwaves and appear to be growing stronger every day. This infuriates liberals and it is even common to hear them rant about their disputes with conservative talk radio hosts on the floor of Congress. Did you get that? The floor of Congress!

Now I enjoy conservative talk radio and, due to the domination taking place in this forum, there is a plethora of personalities who have something to offer. In case you have never turned the dial of your radio from the music channels, let me recommend some possibilities in talk radio. Sean Hannity is a feisty, headstrong radio host who never seems to back down to anyone. Michael Savage and the *Savage Nation* is somewhat of an outsider among his conservative radio contemporaries although he is very entertaining and commands a large audience. I'm sure I could get a lot of opposition about the man with the tendency to scream at liberals with his heavy New York accent; however, quite often I find that he says things I wish I could say but don't from an abundance of self restraint. Bill O'Reilly is an interesting libertarian and, save his stand on manmade global warming, I agree with most of what he has to say. His advocacy and work behind *Jessica's Law,* a powerful upgrade to punishments for sex law violations, is absolutely admirable. This is a short list as there are many more and I discover new radio voices of conservative reason every day as I turn the dial or even peruse the internet. In the back of this book I have created an extensive directory of conservative radio hosts that many may find interesting.

While noticing the many radio personalities who I think make a difference, there is one personality who reigns supreme above the rest — Rush Limbaugh. Self-coined as the "maharushi," Rush has been a national success as well as a perpetual optimist for decades and shows no sign of decline. Limbaugh has the ability to transcend with ease his own personal crisis that would sink many public careers, as well as the ability to deflect attacks from liberals, including leading Democrats. An utter stroke of genius that most certainly will ensure that Limbaugh will be hated by liberal Democrats for years to come was in the Harry Reid attack letter of 2007. Democrat Harry Reid sent the infamous letter to Mark Mays, the CEO of Clear Channel Communications, with over 40 Democrat signatures attempting to silence the verbose radio host. Limbaugh took the letter and placed it on eBay with a pledge to match the purchase amount and send all the funds to the Marine Corps-Law Enforcement Foundation (Limbaugh, 2007). Not only did Limbaugh get tremendous public support for his claim that the Reid letter was an unfair attempt to silence him, but the letter sold for a tremendous $2,100,100 to a Betty Casey, trustee of the Eugene D. Casey Foundation (Limbaugh, 2007). All in all, the foundation received $4.2 million dollars (Limbaugh, 2007). This crafty maneuvering by Limbaugh turned the tables on Democrats and is another example of the characteristic craftiness that has been a Limbaugh trademark his entire career.

I chose Rush Limbaugh as an example of a potential victim of the Democrat move to re-implement the unconstitutional Fairness Doctrine. Of course, the Fairness Doctrine, proclaimed by Democrats as a law to level the playing field on what information is disseminated on the airwaves is, in reality, a tool to limit the market's demand for conservative talk radio. That's right, the free market works for thoughts as well as physical products and, if you don't believe me, just ask the folks that run liberal radio such as Air America — they're bankrupt. I received a tremendous reader response on this article which included government officials and their staff, as well as lay people from the U.S. and internationally. Again, humor was the weapon of choice in the article but the message is completely serious. That is, when you take away the free market for ideological thought as well as physical products, you've started down the fast track to socialism.

Seven Minutes of Limbaugh

As a growing debate builds over a Democrat inspired push to resurrect the Fairness Doctrine and artificially decrease the market demand for conservative radio, there may be no better time to pay homage to one of the stalwart radio personalities that personifies the conservative dominance of the airwaves. That individual is Rush Limbaugh. I have been a Rush Limbaugh listener for many years. As my daily schedule has altered, as does often happen in life, I would listen to different segments of the daily program and enjoy the creative educational environment that Rush seems to create with ease and grace. I would always listen to at least an hour of the show, even in the most hectic of daily schedules, until at one point in my life I found myself in the most peculiar of situations. Yes, that is when a strange and powerful set of forces came together that both limited and increased for me the phenomenon that is known as the Rush Limbaugh experience.

Let me quickly set the stage. You see, I am one of America's more oppressed minority groups today. I am a conservative in academia. I am one of those people who enjoys studying and you will most often find me with my nose in a book or behind a computer terminal. From a pure learning aspect, college is a wonderful place. However, it is from the downsides of college that my story is born.

While I have been fortunate to have studied under several excellent professors, and even a few conservatives in hiding, this is not always the general rule of academia. If you are a conservative and have had the opportunity and privilege to go to college, then you know it to be moreover a liberal horde. With the possible exclusion of my current environment, I have found that it makes little difference if you are attending college in the northeast, the heartland, or in the deep south of the U.S., a great majority of professors in university settings literally drip liberalism.

Of course, the student is a captive of the classroom when instructors decide to stray from teaching to preaching socialistic liberal doctrine. The student learns quickly that the liberal compassion doled out to students by professors who are questioned in the classroom is a tricky and dangerous thing. While some professors are very fair, questioning the liberal spew brought forth by others in the classroom is akin to handling poisonous snakes; that is, inevitably you will get bit and it will cause you pain. So the conservative student picks carefully his battles in the classroom.

I can tell you from experience that curbing ones discontent at the repetitious attempts by some professors to conduct liberal indoctrination in the classroom can at times be draining and stressful. For me, that is where Rush has often come in to save the day. After hours of hearing "America is bad, Reagan was the devil, and Michael Moore is a legitimate research source" nothing was more soothing than a solid hour, if not more, of the "maharushi." For me, listening to the Rush Limbaugh program serves as a mental detoxification that helps to cleanse the mind and invigorate the body for the rest of what is often a full and taxing day of higher learning.

It was in testing the limits of the "Power of Rush" that I came to analyze and develop a new understanding of why Rush Limbaugh has remained the most popular conservative radio host in America. My own personal field analysis was not of my own choosing. Some time back, I found myself in a class schedule that all but bypassed the Rush program. What had previously been hours of afternoon study time turned into wall-to-wall classes with only fifteen minutes of freedom. What kind of impact could Rush have on my day in fifteen minutes? If that's not enough, the challenge would increase.

Due to the fact that most structures within academia are constructed to reject conservative airwaves, I had to descend two flights of stairs daily and exit a building to listen to the program. Furthermore, after subtracting periodic profit center announcements, I found myself with a narrow window of seven minutes of pure Limbaugh. They say that absence makes the heart grow fonder, and that may be true. However, I found in my daily seven-minute meeting with the man behind the golden EIB microphone, some fundamental aspects that embody the entire program. I also believe that they are the keys to the Limbaugh success story.

Within seven minutes, Rush will forward several timely issues of the day, raise my blood pressure, and then bring me back down by making me laugh. Make no doubt about it, Rush is a conservative warrior who is out to win the battle of ideologies by serving up the truth whether you agree with him or not; however, his ability to periodically make fun of the issues we all tend to stress out over not only refocuses the mind, but tends to build a level of endearment for the messenger. With all the pessimism that is strategically forced on the public by the liberal media today, Rush is a breath of fresh air.

For me, Rush's entire program is centered on the idea that there is an important battle being fought in America, a battle for the hearts and minds of Americans. The future of this country depends on the victory of traditional conservative values over the liberal socialistic ideals that challenge for supremacy. Rush does more than articulate his optimistic belief that conservatives will win the day, he literally exudes optimism. In my opinion, this is Rush Limbaugh's strongest attribute. What might be as interesting as the existence of all these qualities is that Rush can demonstrate them all with flare and grace in seven minutes flat. So, while Democrats once again strategize to gain ground they can't earn with a rebirth of the Fairness Doctrine, it seems only fitting to recognize a true victorious warrior of the airwaves, and that warrior is Rush Limbaugh. (Ibbetson, 2007, July 21)

References

Armstrong, C. *Religion of Violence*. Printed by permission of author.

Ibbetson, P. A. (2007, July 21). Seven Minutes of Limbaugh. *Canada Free Press*. Retrieved from http://www.canadafreepress.com/2007/ ibbetson072007.htm

Ibbetson, P. A. (2007, October 15). Death of a messenger. *Capitol Hill Coffee House*. Retrieved from http://capitolhillcoffeehouse.com/ more.php?id=4231_0_1_0_M

Limbaugh, R. (2007, October 19). *Betty Casey wins smear letter at $2,100,100; Rush matches bid; MC-LEF will get a total of $4.2 M*. Retrieved December 22, 2007, from http://www.rushlimbaugh. com/home/daily/site_101907/content/01125110.guest.html

Chapter 3

Jackals and Monkeys

WHEN WE TALK ABOUT JACKALS and monkeys we are talking about very different animals with their own unique mannerisms and modes of operation. For our purposes in the zoo of life observations we are undertaking, I wish to make clear how those two animals fit into the political landscape of today.

The first would be the jackal. Jackals are a conniving bunch of scavengers who will eat the half rotten corpse of just about any animal as a meal of opportunity. These marauding hooligans are on the constant lookout for the old, the weak, as well as the very young in the herd to exploit at a moment's notice. When the jackals are about, an unfortunate injury or bout of sickness on the part of a member of the herd may be all the jackal needs to gain advantage in a striking attack. In this chapter I identify three jackals in the political world today: Michael Moore, Rosa Brooks, and the Westboro Baptist Church.

For many years Michael Moore has been gnawing at the foundations of this country one anti-American documentary at a time. Let's put this into perspective. We all make up this country and even Michael Moore, with his love for Canada, is still included. The problem is that Michael Moore has found he can make a living under the capitalist system by catering to left wing socialists who would like to turn this country upside down. I believe the majority of the country sees him for what he is but, like a clever jackal, Moore has more than filled his belly by selling a loathsome product that undermines the goodness of this country. The product, which is sold under the guise of improving America, is nothing short of absolute lies. Before you read the article on Moore that was one of the most read for June 2007 on the *New Media Journal*, we had better talk a little bit about monkeys.

Monkeys by and large are a humorous lot with their silly antics and entertaining ways. Of course, if you have been to the zoo you will know that monkeys are not above pitching a ball of excrement your way and so one must keep an eye on the silly monkey as well as being able to identify poo as poo. One of the saddest things I think a trip to the zoo demonstrates is that life there, like life in the real world, is quite often not fair and, despite the signage, there is often someone who wants to degrade the animals with a bit of food and false kindness. Monkeys are a sucker for this and they can be made to do the most degrading things for some scraps and a smile.

Thus enters Cindy Sheehan. Don't misinterpret my feelings for Cindy Sheehan. She is probably more victim than perpetrator in the role she has played, or the role she has been coaxed into playing in the opposition of the Bush administration. First, Sheehan was a grieving mother of a fallen soldier in which she shared a common bond with many mothers in this country. What followed next was nothing short of a circus ride of follies that saw the aggrieved Cindy Sheehan morph from a liberal Bush basher to communist sympathizer, from sad mother to incoherent mad hatter. What many may have missed during the frolicking spins and tumbles of the Sheehan debacle was that she was at all times being prodded and poked, coaxed and cajoled, by a liberal media that used her as a convenient tool to attack President Bush and a war they did not support. Don't agree? Think about it. Where is Cindy Sheehan now? Is she out of the political world? We can ask this question because, for the most part, her face has disappeared from the media spotlight. The answer is that she is still quite active but is now fighting Democrats because she believes they failed their promise to end the Iraq war. You see, the monkey is now performing the wrong tricks and the liberal media is no longer happy to reward the performance. Sheehan must be accountable for her statements and actions against her own country in a time of war; however, these judgments must also be tempered within the knowledge that she was taken advantage of by the liberal media while in a weak mental state. I have heard people within academia, as well as other liberal circles, say that Sheehan is an inspiration — a movement leader — who brought about a dialogue about the ills of war. I can only shake my head when I hear such things as I think of Sheehan as a tragic story of a grieving mother who was tricked into playing the role of the "silly monkey."

Michael Moore: A Criminal Profile

There is little doubt that Michael Moore is one of the most public anti-American propagandists of modern times. Without fail, his lengthy lists of so called documentary works have all encompassed his varying visions of the shortcomings of the United States. What many Americans take issue with Moore is the deceptive means by which he collects his information, and the even more deceptive way he portrays this information to the public.

When lamenting about Moore's last work, *Fahrenheit 9/11*, Christopher Hitchens would say, 'To describe this film as dishonest and demagogic would almost be to promote those terms to the level of respectability. To describe this film as a piece of crap would be to run the risk of a discourse that would never again rise above the excremental... *Fahrenheit 9/11* is a sinister exercise in moral frivolity, crudely disguised as an exercise in seriousness. It is also a spectacle of abject political cowardice masking itself as a demonstration of "dissenting" bravery.' (Hitchens, 2004, ¶3).

Hitchens' observation is important to the profiling of Moore for two reasons. First, he encapsulates a general feeling of many Americans and, more importantly, it shows that even the most godless among us realize that there is something fundamentally wrong with Michael Moore. Dave Kopel, of the Independence Institute, who appears in the Michael Moore rebuttal film *Fahrenhype 9/11*, has chronicled 59 falsehoods within Moore's documentary.

Hitchens and countless others have been able to touch upon the modus operandi of Moore which includes an overabundance of lies and trickery. Examples of trickery include ambushing politicians trying to make their way into government buildings, and the lowly deception in *Bowling for Columbine* of pretending to be a Second Amendment advocate to get into Charlton Hesston's home to verbally attack the aged actor for his kindness. Moore has used his abilities in "cut and paste" respondent editing to make a mockery of the truth and cater to the far left anti-American crowd. It should also be mentioned that he has made a fortune in the process.

However, realizing that Michael Moore is an America hater who lies, is only observing the symptoms of what truly makes the man what he is. To have an adequate profile of Moore, a person must understand why he does what he does.

First, it must be understood that Moore is not a dupe or lackey. To compare Moore with dim-witted pawns of the Democratic Party, such as Cindy Sheehan, is to make a serious under-estimation of Moore's intelligence. For everything Moore is, he is not stupid. While this may sound like a compliment, it's far from it. Moore's full mental capabilities exempt himself from the forgiveness that some will extend to the Sheehan types of the world.

While it is no doubt true that Moore benefits from the socialist movement within the Democratic Party, he is also not a gun for hire. Moore and the Democratic left simply have similar aims at the moment and this is a point of confusion for many people. When we see Michael Moore sitting in the place of distinction with Jimmy Carter at the 2004 Democratic convention, we are not seeing Michael Moore, the faithful soldier of the Democratic Party, what we are really seeing is Michael Moore representing Michael Moore, Inc. It is here that we can observe the beginnings of the true sociopathic nature of Moore.

What's confusing to most people is that when we think of the sociopath, visions of stone cold killers like Ted Bundy come to mind, not plump loud mouths from Michigan. However, it is the nature of the sociopath that makes Moore a perfect Goebbels style propagandist.

The sociopath is void of a standard conscience and is not limited in personal action due to feelings of guilt. If this individual can attain what he/she wants, the means to that end have no relevance. Being seen as a hypocrite or dishonest carries no weight past what formal sanctions can bring. When Michael Moore attacks Dick Cheney for his affiliation to Halliburton, while owning stock himself, there are no pangs of guilt or remorse, only frustration at being exposed. Moore, as a sociopath, is free to attack the war effort as well as the survival of the country for his own personal gain with impunity.

Sociopaths are highly functional. While they do not feel bound to general moral codes, they do realize that to stay free in society, to continue the quest for their personal gratification, they must appear to conform to societal norms. Sociopaths are often identified by the public by their personal indulgences that are so deviant from societal norms they require incarceration or elimination.

For instance, Ted Bundy was highly functional and blended well in the society until his desire to destroy the flesh eventually identified himself as a sociopath. In contrast to Ted Bundy, Moore's personal indulgence is simply to line his pockets by undermining the country. While the damage Moore brings to the U.S. in lowering national morale, reinforcing the warped conceptions of America by socialist countries around the world, and encouraging America's enemies, may in the long run cause a loss of life greater than Bundy's, its immediate effects are less obvious.

The point that people should be brought to understand is that if the fates had placed Moore in a communist country, he would most likely be undermining that system for his personal gain by any means he could muster. Ironic isn't it?

There is no doubt that the public will receive another large dose of the same old same old with Moore's new labor of love, *Sicko*. However, as Moore promotes Cuba's communistic medical program, people should be armed with the knowledge that what they are seeing is not the work of a naïve communist convert, but the cold calculations of a sociopathic mind. (Ibbetson, 2007, June 9)

While many people found the Moore article thought provoking, if not illuminating, the usual liberal onslaught that follows an article such as this came full force. I am not one to shy away from a debate on anything I write, and I argued with many angry liberals who were literally frothing at the mouth to defend the documentary creator. The issue might have been laid to rest but, like a jelly-of-the-month subscription or, more accurately, a case of genital warts, Michael Moore is the gift that just keeps on giving. On the eve of the 2008 Republican National Convention, Michael Moore would validate my criminal profile with some of the most villainous wishes for New Orleans that have been uttered to date. Dutifully, I wrote about it.

Gustav, God, and Michael Moore: Validations of a Criminal Profile

In the summer of 2007, I constructed a profile and analysis on Michael Moore which illuminated the sociopathic tendencies that encompass the actions of one of the most infamous documentary creators of modern times. Within the article, *Michael Moore: A Criminal Profile*, which was first released in the *New Media Journal* and then later around the world, I took careful pains to make sure that readers understood that Moore carries the tendencies of the sociopath while not accusing him of the crimes that some sociopaths actually commit. The thrust of the article was to introduce people to the moral wasteland in which the sociopath lives and operates. Of course, this caused somewhat of a ruckus among Moore lackeys and those who enjoy the anti-American sales pitch he throws out with each new theatrical falsehood he creates. Unfortunately, for those who wish to defend Moore, for whatever their motivation, there is one factor they will never be able to overcome — the mouth of Michael Moore.

On August 29, 2008, on MSNBC with Keith Olbermann, Michael Moore would make one of his most inflammatory statements to date — he would thank God that Hurricane Gustav might hit New Orleans and the Gulf Coast region. Moore's joy was centered on the notion that the life threatening hurricane would be politically damaging to the 2008 Republican National Convention. Let's get real for a moment about what's really happening with a statement like this from Moore. Some would say, in defense of Moore, that he may have been unduly bolstered into making a statement as outlandish as this due to the fact that he was in the presence of the well known Bush attack dog Keith Olbermann. I would warn against selling Michael Moore short in this manner. As I did in 2007, I would again say that Michael Moore is not a dupe or a follower. On the contrary, as a sociopath, Moore is cool and calculated and does not require the validation of anyone to have self fulfillment, including cohorts in similar Bush bashing causes such as Olbermann. As with the sociopath, Moore understands that Olbermann, as well as potential natural disasters like Hurricane Gustav, can be of benefit to the only real concern that a sociopath has — him or herself. Does Moore want dead bodies and billons in property damage as was seen in Hurricane Katrina? Perhaps not. However, the bottom line, and it's just as dirty, is that Moore, like the sociopath, just doesn't really care what happens if he benefits in the end.

If we observe the macabre conversation between Moore and Olbermann on the desires of the day for Hurricane Gustav, we notice that after having a hearty laugh over New Orleans taking the brunt of another hurricane following the devastating Katrina, Moore, after the fact, states that he is not looking for human casualties in the mix of his deadly desires. This is a very late form of quality control in his conversation with Olbermann and, looking at the totality of the conversation, it appears to be stated only halfheartedly. To give an equivalent of Moore's Gustav statement to readers from the heartland of this country is like saying, "I pray to God a tornado falls on your house, because it would be really good for me if it did…but I hope it does not cause you any major problems." Yep, it doesn't take an overabundance of brain power to come to the conclusion that people don't rate very high in comparison to Moore's own desires and wishes. The point of Moore's Gustav statement goes beyond showing that he is simply a jerk, what it does is tie this newest public statement into an intricate web of Moore's activities of many years that shows specific psychological components of the mindset of the "me first," "me at any cost" mentality. This is a unique characteristic of the sociopath who cares nothing about the people around him or her and, in the case of Moore, the country in which he lives.

Moore has gone to great expense to frame himself as the kindly rotund truth talker of American inadequacies. Many still buy into this fairytale, and those people will surely be angry at my words. I feel no joy in angering them as I felt no joy in documenting Moore's sociopathic profile in 2007. That is, sometimes being right does not bring adulation, smiles, and applause. What it does is forward the truth and brings it to the light of day and, in the end, possibly, gives people a new perspective in which to evaluate an operator like Michael Moore. (Ibbetson, 2008, September 8)

Now some jackals are not of the sociopathic nature. Some are intellectuals, you know, the "Grey Poupon passers" of the world. Living in the ivory towers of their own minds, they wish, if only for a moment, to toss down a nugget of their infinite knowledge to the great unwashed masses. That's probably the grandiose version. In reality, they just want others to share their own warped views of this country. The article below was a rebuttal to a *L.A. Times* column by liberal writer and academic Rosa Brooks who thought it only wise to impart to readers that we have an unwarranted number of undeserving heroes in the War on Terror. This is what I call a Grey Poupon jackal at work. Smart enough to know that the country would never go for saying that military service is worthless, sacrifice for your fellow American is a waste of time, or that defending the greatest nation on earth is wrong, Brooks, like the jackal, circles to the rear flanks of the herd. Instead she says that she endorses heroes but with an unreachable criteria of requirements. As a strong military supporter, as an America loving citizen, as a person with more than two brain cells to rub together, I took offense at her article and answered back. I did so with an analysis of Brooks as well as the "I can" philosophy that I believe not only embodies the great men and women of the military, but also is an inherent part of the American spirit. Take that Rosa Brooks!

"I can…," a Conservative Philosophy

Every great movement and accomplishment that has taken place in America, even those supported by thousands of people, was at its most basic inception born of a single individual who said, "I can." Those who stood up first when others remained seated and said, "I can make a difference, I can fight for what's right, I can help those in need," and the list goes on and on. As surely as birds of a feather flock together, the "I cans" of this country find each other when their services are needed and, like magic, the "I can" philosophy is transformed into the "we can" philosophy and grand innovations are conceived, wonders of construction are built, epic battles are won, and heroes are born.

I was perplexed to read the August 3, 2007, article, "Heroism and the Language of Fascism" by Rosa Brooks, in the *Los Angeles Times*, as her inaccuracies of what makes a hero simply demean a populace least likely to call her to task. I'm talking about real heroes. Brooks alludes that former NFL star Pat Tillman does not meet her criteria of a hero, at least in part, because the bullet that took his life was a product of friendly fire. This line of thinking goes beyond petty and straight to pathetic. Think about it for a moment. Tillman left the lavish life and monetary rewards of the NFL to go to a place where people want to kill you, where death walks with you all day, every day. No Rosa, Tillman was not shot by Osama bin Laden while wrestling a rhino to save a hospital full of babies, but he did go to Iraq when his NFL compatriots stayed safely behind and, despite the dangers, he gave the ultimate sacrifice on the battlefield for his country. Why? Because Tillman was an "I can" man, the fundamental building block of what heroes are made of and the clear delineation between conservative and liberal thought today. Of course, if you exclude service, sacrifice, and suffering on the battlefield as a pre-requisite for heroism, as Brooks requires, you can probably exclude everyone.

Brooks attempts to cloud the issue by saying that the few true heroes of today are not heralded while legions of the unworthy are given all the glory. After generally disparaging the military, along with all the emergency services, she insults everyone's intelligence by telling readers that she really has respect for the groups she has proclaimed unfit to be called heroes. In doing so, Brooks assumes that readers have the mental capacity of an acorn which simply adds insult to injury when reading her article.

Knowing that people will most likely see her analysis as liberal tripe, Brooks prepares to be rejected, if not ran out of town, by those who hold the military and emergency services dear. I would admit that this was the knee-jerk reaction that came to my mind as well. However, as a former law enforcement officer, I learned a long time ago that simply running out of town those who would undermine, if not hurt society, simply passes the problem on to another city. It is always better to expose and deal with folks like Brooks directly, despite the human nature to simply reject them and move on. You might call it going above and beyond the call of duty.

What we see with the Brooks analysis is simply another version of the same old liberal defeat policy. Yes, these are the "I can'ts" of the Democratic party. Those who scream by their actions and statements, "I can't support America, I can't seek victory," and, of course, Brooks' I can't handle too many heroes in a time of war.

While conservatives fight to ensure the future of this nation, the "I can'ts" have consistently been sowing the seeds of pessimism and defeat. Some shout defeatist rhetoric from the activist picket lines while others, fancying themselves more clever, attempt to sell the idea that an over abundance of heroes in a time of war is the equivalent of the beginnings of a communist nation. Are you buying it? This is the big question, because as I stated earlier, the victims of Brooks' hero stripping philosophy will not be the ones most likely to challenge her. The police officers, fire fighters, and military men and women are trained to routinize even the most heroic acts as part of their jobs. While those on the outside of this work sometimes find it strange, in reality it is a very practical policy as it helps to rationalize what is often extremely stressful work and stabilize normal men and women to have careers that most can't begin to fathom. Rosa Brooks has more than proven she is part of that latter group.

Unfortunately, simply exposing the liberal defeat policy of Brooks is not enough. It is the responsibility of all conservatives who do not wear the uniform to avoid being led astray on this issue, and to champion those who have stepped forward and are fighting and dying for our freedom. This is most certainly a time for "extraordinary courage, fortitude and greatness of soul," and a most necessary time for the gathering of those embracing the conservative philosophy of "I can..." (Ibbetson, 2007, August 13)

I saved the worst jackal of all for last. This is a rabid beast so vile and re-pulsive that even the normal opportunistic jackal will not allow it within its pack. This creature, while sharing many scavenger-like qualities, is forced by its overly repugnant nature to hunt alone, and that's exactly what it does. In my writings I have dealt with the good, the bad, and the liberal; however, I have found few that could turn my stomach to the degree of the Westboro Baptist Church. The Westboro Baptist Church, while physically no more than a sorry little band of cult members holding a quaint little compound in the state of Kansas, have brought pain to people from sea to shining sea with a sadistic philosophy that your pain is Westboro's righteous gain. I wrote the following article dealing with the Westboro Baptist Church for every military family that has had to suffer the demented ridicule of this band of cultish misfits while attempting to bury their husband, daughter, son, or wife. For me, the article was in part an apology to military families from a member of the state of Kansas; in part a bold clarification of reality to readers as a Christian, a religion which the Westboroers have viciously misportrayed; and lastly an attempt by a proud American to draw the line in the sand in the face of a scourge and say "I have had enough!" You can decide for yourself if I hit the mark in any of these attempts.

Westboro Baptist Church: The Scourge of the Flatlands

When I think of my home state of Kansas, I think of a place where people are friendly, work hard, and moreover believe in the Christian values that this great nation was founded upon. I have always thought that the Kansas designation as part of the Bible belt was a badge of honor that many of the blue states just don't often understand. However, there has been for some time a pestilence walking the flatlands of Kansas, a scourge that brings only pain and sorrow to all who find themselves within its path. I am talking about the members of the Westboro Baptist Church. The Westboro Baptist Church, which comprises the immediate family of Fred Phelps, is based out of Topeka, Kansas, and have made it their mission to spread a twisted religious philosophy of God's damnation on the world one protest at a time.

I ran across the Phelps clan a few years ago when they were protesting a church I was attending in Wichita, Kansas. I had never heard of the group before and I suddenly found myself within swinging distance without any context of who I was dealing with. I assumed from their colorful "GOD HATES FAGS" signs that they were a pro-homosexual advocacy group possibly angry about a Bible lesson on Sodom and Gomorrah that they might have heard at the church that did not fit their lifestyle. I later found that the Westboro Baptist Church was a small, crazy, dysfunctional family group turned cult that liked to travel to the funerals of dead soldiers to tell their families that their child was in hell due to the evils of homosexuality. These acts of lunacy and open displays of pure hate earned the Westboro Baptist Church the designation as a hate group by the Southern Poverty Law Center, a designation that these folks have worked hard to earn.

Some might ask the question, why give this group any recognition? Is it not recognition that they seek? Is this not why this group will protest any event that brings more than three people together? I have thought hard about this because there are some valid truths to these questions. However, I think silence can also be construed as a validation. Silence can also be seen as a weakness. It seems to me that many in Kansas have been using silence as the weapon of choice against Fred Phelps and family for far too long. Like disregarding a cancerous tumor in the hopes that it will die off by itself, the death of the entire body is the most likely result. The reality is that the tumor must be removed and this is always bloody work. Listening to the boastful exclamations of Fred Phelps when he says that his cult group has performed 30,000 protests in the last 17 years with no signs of slowing down brings me to a reality that this group has to be dealt with.

What do I mean by that? Aren't the Phelps group afforded the same free speech rights that I have to disseminate this article? The ACLU, who always jumps to the aid of those who would undermine this country, says so. In reality, the ACLU's aid to the Phelps clan, which is part of the selective aid the organization gives those that they wish to assist, reflects only the anti-American agenda of the ACLU, not the championing of free speech. The reasons the Phelps congregation has no legal right to vomit their hatred of America upon military families in mourning is that hate speech has no protection under the Constitution. The October 31, 2007, civil ruling against the group which amounted to the original sum of $11 million in damages is an example of the courts' ability to distinguish free speech from the willful intention to inflict emotional distress on the families of fallen American soldiers. Now that was a happy day.

For Kansas, the Phelps cult makes our progressive state appear mindless, backward, and racist. Those who would like to continue the stereotypes often identified with small rural states simply need to inject the Phelps cult into the debate. For Christians in general, the Westboro Baptist Church is a blight on the name of true religion. When Christians tackle the true social issues that face this country they must not only battle the secular liberal opposition that is always prevalent but also the damage to the credibility of Christian values itself brought forth by the evil labors of the Westboro Baptist Church.

Lastly, the war effort itself is undermined by the treasonous acts of protests by this group. While legislation has been adopted to raise the penalties for funeral protests, this is only a mild rebuke compared to past wartime legislation toward treasonous acts. It is in this arena that I believe further action should be explored.

Over the long haul, Kansas will survive having these folks in their state, the good will win over the bad. Over the long haul, judgment will be handed down by a higher power for all of us including the Phelps clan. I could lament about the special place in hell I believe the members of the Westboro Baptist Church will be given, but it would add nothing new from what so many others in this country have already thought of before me. Over the long haul, the United States will continue to champion freedom and protect this country by way of the proud men and women who serve and sometimes make the ultimate sacrifice to keep us safe. What do we, the American people, who are protected every minute of the day by men and women of the military, owe to them as they are being heckled and verbally damned as they are laid to rest? You see, it's not that legal action should be taken against the Westboro Baptist Church to simply restore the greatness of Kansas, or the true nature of Christianity, or even for the protection of the families of fallen soldiers to have peaceful, respectful funerals. I would submit that it is because of the culmination of all three of these factors that the time is now for the collective effort of all Americans to call for the end of the mission of hate brought forth by the Westboro Baptist Church. (Ibbetson, 2008, February 12)

Now some folks have combined the hybrid nature of the silly monkey and devilish jackal. That is, they throw their poop in the eyes of America and then circle around to bite those who stop long enough to wipe away the excrement. I could not think of anyone who fit this depiction more perfectly than MSNBC's Keith Olbermann. I think my article says it all. Enjoy.

31

The Five Follies of Keith Olbermann

For some time now a struggling MSNBC has employed a Bush hating mad hatter by the name of Keith Olbermann. Olbermann appears to be on an endless mission to disparage the President as well as the War on Terror, and in doing so has created a very interesting example of the inner workings of the far left liberal. First, in highlighting the five follies of Olbermann, it is only fair to give the disclaimer that these failings are not Olbermann's alone but are general characteristics of the far left. Keith Olbermann is recognized for analysis because he showcases these characteristics beyond what the average angry liberal is capable of due to his platform as a talking head at MSNBC. Secondly, there must be some observance given to the actions of Olbermann that must be placed within the context of the highly competitive environment of the political news world in which Olbermann lives and in which he must contend with competitors, such as Bill O'Reilly, who are consistently besting him in the ratings. To avoid any misconception that excuses are being made for individuals such as Olbermann, the five follies which make up the angry liberal are submitted:

1. Acts of the demented;
2. The jack-in-the-box syndrome;
3. The conspiracy theorist;
4. The birds of a feather showcase; and
5. The forked tongue debilitation.

First and foremost Olbermann's presentation to the public carries a constant appearance of the unhinged, whether it is the anger filled shaking of his body as he rants at President Bush or the wild-eyed glint of the madman when he is in full verbal contortion. Almost every show with Keith Olbermann is akin to a trip to the psycho ward. The jack-in-the-box syndrome; that is, the mindless repetition of the same old scripted performance which usually begins and ends with "Bush lied," is without a doubt a fundamental component of Olbermann's inability to reach higher echelons of popularity. Now, for amusement's sake,

Olbermann's constant performance as the dysfunctional "Sherlock Holmes," the man who alone appears to constantly unearth the criminal acts of the President is good for a few laughs but, upon continual repetition, places his credibility alongside the 9-11 truthers, Code Pink, and the Westboro Baptist Church to name a few.

They say that you can know a person by the people they run with and Olbermann's chummy nature and growing contribution list for the ultra radical Daily Kos has made it abundantly clear who he has made his closest bedfellows. Yes, birds of a feather do flock together and Olbermann and the Daily Kos make for some very dirty birds. Last, but not least, Olbermann suffers from an extreme case of the forked tongue debilitation. That's right, he is just plain and simply a liar. Pulling baseless fabrication after fabrication out of the air, Keith Olbermann paints a false picture of the President and the War on Terror that the word "shameful" cannot fully describe.

The five follies of Olbermann describe an individual whose actions are not duplicated on any of the other cable news networks regardless of the political slants that may or may not be present to viewers as they turn their television dial. In short, Keith Olbermann is the most overt activist for the left in the media today and his equivalent counterpart on the right is yet to be created, and I hope it never is. I am sure that some birds of a similar feather will come to the defense of Olbermann after reading this article, but I challenge them to defend the five follies of Olbermann, for to do so they will have to become Olbermann, and that is truly scary business. MSNBC has made their bed with Olbermann and it is a testament to the direction they appear to want to go with their organization, and that's fine, it's a big world and there will always be folks like that out there. Meanwhile, other networks, such as FOX, will continue to collect the bountiful rewards of MSNBC's tactical decision to encourage by employment the follies of Keith Olbermann. (Ibbetson, 2008, June 12)

References

Hitchens, C. (2004, June 21). Unfairenheit 9/11, the lies of Michael Moore. *Slate*. Retrieved June 2, 2007, from http://www.slate.com/id/2102723/

Ibbetson, P. A. (2007, June 9). Michael Moore: A criminal profile. *New Media Journal*. Retrieved from http://www.newmediajournal.us/guest/p_ibbetson/06092007.htm

Ibbetson, P. A. (2007, August 13). "I can...," a conservative philosophy. *Renew America*. Retrieved from http://www.renewamerica.us/columns/ibbetson/070813

Ibbetson, P. A. (2008, February 12). Westboro Baptist Church: The scourge of the flatlands. *Renew America*. Retrieved from http://www.renewamerica.us/columns/ibbetson/080212

Ibbetson, P. A. (2008, June 12). The five follies of Keith Olbermann. *Capitol Hill Coffee House*. Retrieved from http://capitolhillcoffeehouse.com/more.php?id=5481_0_1_0_M

Ibbetson, P. A. (2008, September 8). Gustav, God, and Michael Moore: Validations of a criminal profile. *MichNews.com*. Retrieved from http://www.michnews.com/artman/publish/article_21172.shtml

Kopel, D. (2004). Fifty-nine deceits in Fahrenheit 9/11. *Dave Kopel*. Retrieved June 3, 2007, from www.davekopel.org/Terror/Fiftysix-Deceits-in-Fahrenheit-911.htm

Chapter 4

Straight Talk and Straight Thought

WHEN IT COMES TO THE conservative philosophy, it is my belief that everyone has to take their own road. What I mean is it's not my goal to try to make readers believe like me. I would rather inspire people to think for themselves and to question a lot of the garbage, such as political correctness, that is being pushed on them than say "live by my playbook of life."

Now I have a philosophy and, of course, I think I'm right. This book is a compilation of my beliefs and thoughts on what I believe are fundamentally important issues that affect our country. If I did not think they were important I would not share them. I have received an enormous response, sometimes positive and sometimes negative, on the issues I write about. The bottom line is that you may find yourself in agreement with me on some issues or you may not, but if you're mulling over issues that you previously paid no attention to, and thinking for yourself (yes, I said thinking), then that is where this book is supposed to take you.

I believe that most people embody the fundamental conservative principles of life and don't know it. What are these principles? Well, they are often foreshadowed by political issues that are falsely portrayed as Republican issues. In fact, political parties have nothing to do with the tenets of conservatism and it is easy to assume that one party is conservative and the other is liberal or be lulled into giving false support and opposition to parties which may have nothing to do with supporting conservative values. We will come back to that in a moment.

In its most simplistic form, conservatism can be found under these three basic principles: (1) God, (2) Family, and (3) Country. While some might say that this is overly simplistic, there is a tremendous amount wrapped in these three principles. Think about it.

Fundamentally, conservatives believe in the existence of a God and his son Jesus Christ. They believe in the existence of God's holy word contained in the Bible. The Bible is considered the divine message from the Lord to his people and the only divine text from which to guide one's life. Conservatives believe in a judgment day when people will be called to account for their actions on this earth. Conservatives believe that salvation comes from an individual relationship with God and a personal acceptance of the Lord as their Savior followed by his divine grace and forgiveness.

Conservatives believe in the sacredness of the traditional family unit. They believe the holy values of marriage, that being between a man and woman, and the responsibility to raise children with knowledge and respect for the Lord first, and then their fellow citizens. While it would seem that the next would be obvious, the environment we live in today makes it paramount to state that the conservative principles of God and family make the unborn, known by God before birth, sacred. Simply put, abortion is nothing short of murder. No further clarification should be needed on this issue.

The recognized value, respect, and love for country is the third principle of conservatism. While much of the power of conservative principles is in its lack of needless nuance and vagueness, it is important here to make sure that there is no confusion about love of country. The conservative support for this country does not mean that they do not support change. It does not mean that they (myself included) do not see flaws in this country, or avenues for the country's improvement. What it does mean is that the basic foundational elements of this country created by the founding fathers: the Bill of Rights, the Constitution, the Christian foundation, the free market, and the need for small government should be maintained and protected. These Christian tenets of conservatism may have some variations but, generally speaking, this is the conservative view.

Now you may be thinking that I have not addressed such pertinent issues as taxes, border security, global warming, the War on Terror, gay marriage, abortion and the list goes on and on and on. My answer is that these are political issues which are of themselves separate from conservatism and liberalism; that is, they are issues that are dealt with by individuals who make their decisions based on a conservative or liberal philosophy. You know, those lovely politicians.

By and large, liberals come to a fundamental point of contention on all three points of conservatism. Moral relativism, often called secular humanism, which is now an ingrained liberal philosophy since the 1960s, calls to question the existence of God, the usefulness of the traditional family, and lastly, the viability of the capitalistic system. If left to their devices, liberals would turn this country on its head looking for the unattainable Marxian utopia. I cannot stress enough, while history shows us that all the previous attempts to incorporate Marxism have created totalitarian governments that produced nothing but death in great quantities, there has been a failure by conservatives today to properly articulate to the American people just how damaging this failed philosophy is, and that it remains a threat today.

In our country, socialism and communism have for some time been nipping at the heels of our capitalistic system. It would be folly of the greatest consequence to not believe that even in the latter stages of socialism's global exhibition of failure, that the United States is incapable of handing over its place in the world and becoming one in a long line of destitute communistic dictatorships. Some say we are quickly moving in that direction. I believe that the opposition to the fundamental principles of conservatism has been leading us down that road; however, I am optimistic. That optimism is based on my belief that the fundamental principles of conservatism are embraced by the majority, not the minority in this country. This book, in part, addresses issues that many of you conservatives, whether you have ever thought of yourself that way or not, may have pondered but never had someone articulate those ideas in a way that would be useful in a debate with a mouthy liberal.

Let me give you one example of a fundamental difference between conservatives and liberals that is often clouded within the media today. If you were to listen to today's media portrayal of conservatives you would hear, among other things, that conservatives are money hungry capitalists who don't care about the poor and less fortunate. If this were true then it would only be logical that liberals would donate more to the poor and needy, right? Not so. In fact, not only do conservatives give 30% more monetary donations than liberals, they donate considerably more time in labor to what is considered charitable labors (Stossel & Kendall, 2006).

Looking to the fundamentals of conservatism: (1) God, (2) Family, and (3) Country, we see that conservatives, mainly Christians, take upon themselves the individual accountability and direct relationship that is found within Christianity, resulting in a desire for small government. Think about it, if you feel a responsibility for your actions, the need and desire for an over arching government to control and guide will be diminished. Stossel & Kendall (2006) see the differences in donations among conservatives and liberals as a product of differing perceptions of the role of government. I agree as this is in line with the third characteristic of Country.

What I would add is that the three characteristics of conservatism: (1) God, (2) Family, and (3) Country are enmeshed characteristics; that is, one directly affects the other with a specific order of importance. To put it more simply, conservatives donate more money to the poor than liberals for the same reasons they oppose abortion, because they are impacted more to do so by the teachings of God. Furthermore, true conservatism involves adherence to all three characteristics. When someone tells you they are a conservative but support abortion, or they are a conservative but want expanded government in its various forms, you can tell from the onset of that discussion that you are not dealing with a true conservative. That statement is not meant to make you angry, it's simply telling you the truth.

There are a lot of fine folks who champion certain parts and not others of the fundamental characteristics of conservatism that I have laid out. They often do wonderful things for the world and I often support them in their endeavors, but the truth of the matter is that they are not true conservatives. Call them moderates, rhinos, liberals, or any other term that fits your fancy, but conservatives they are not. Readers may not agree with me in full on this matter. They may only agree with me on certain issues or what I have to say may simply stimulate readers to think about issues I have not addressed. Either way we are both winning because we are engaged in individual contemplation, research, and analysis. I am confident that conservatives will immediately see the inherent conflicts within the liberal media, the Democrat Party, and liberals in general. These conflicts violate the fundamental principles and characteristics of conservatism that I have already laid out. From here on, it is appropriate to think of my articles you have already read, and the ones that follow, as being open for your critique for their validity in championing conservative values.

If you are a liberal you have waded through many pages and have read many things that I am sure have offended you to some extent. Unlike Ann Coulter, I feel a little bad for you because the goal is not to hurt you but to save this country if not the soul of this nation. The purpose of this book is to share the conservative philosophy in a politically hostile world and to do so I am prepared to feed the lions. Now don't get me wrong, it's not just you liberals that I consider lions, it's anyone who may take offense to the statements of someone's political beliefs. Funny enough, that's why most of us keep our political beliefs silent, or even worse, train ourselves not to even contemplate a political view because of our belief that it will equal personal pain down the road. Regardless, I encourage the liberal to keep reading whether doing so is an attempt to find one thing you can agree with me on or even if you are just reading because you are gathering information to later attack me with, keep turning those pages. It's not just Christmas when miracles happen and I'm looking for a breakthrough for you folks, too. Shoot, did I just say Christmas? I probably made you guys mad all over again right in the middle of my sales pitch. Oh well, moving on.

Revisiting for a moment the topic of where to place our loyalties, it is important to clear up any other possible misconceptions that the principles of conservatism may create for an individual mulling over these concepts and ideas. First, it must be understood that there are some individuals who fall outside the fundamental principles of conservatism to one degree or another. For example, I personally know a few atheists that are patriots, serve their country, fight against abortion, and on down the line. Are these folks needed in the struggles that face conservatives? The answer is yes. Should they be included within the political tent of the Republican Party or whatever party may house conservatives? I would say absolutely. I would also say that the fundamental principles of conservatism remain sound despite the existence of such anomalous groups. Additionally, a moment of focus should be given to liberals as well. It should always be important for conservatives to separate the liberal philosophy from the individual that adheres to that philosophy. That is, we should never forget that as we fight what is nothing short of a war for the survival of the soul of this country, we are fighting a liberal philosophy first and foremost, not people. If we remove the flawed and fatal philosophy of liberalism from the individual, we are back to people as people and their potential goodness therein.

It is my preference to use analogies in my writings and, quite often, they are in the form of childhood related stories. Some detractors of my work will say that this is beneath the adult reader but I disagree. I believe that childhood stories, if they are related in an honest way, are almost universally understood. To any liberal who might have made it this far into the book, I am not saying that everyone grows up in the same economic situation or that perfect equality exists. What I am saying is, in at least a general way, kids are kids. If you had a brother or sister growing up, you probably share some of the same experiences with other people who had a sibling. Similarly, if you went to public school, you can probably share stories with other public school attendees that have some striking similarities. Because I am trying to convey important messages from a starting point that the majority of us all can relate to, childhood is a friendly place of agreement in which to leap to the adult problems of politics that we tend to fight over vehemently. Most of us would not mind being a kid again if even for a little while.

The Politics of the Playground article was one of the first articles I wrote when I was not aware of word limits and other nuances of the article publishing game. The article was sent back by a lot of publishers who did not just love the piece or maybe my work in general. This article is a *thinker's* piece and also forces the reader to face the *good, bad, and the ugly* of childhood. I guess you could say I am trying to convey the idea that dealing with national security and the real threat of terrorism is not a mystery that we must assume will never really be addressed. These are the words of cowards, who through the mental bombardment of liberalism and its public face, political correctness, have lost or refused to face the most fundamental answers that any child who walks the playground could tell you.

The Politics of the Playground

Currently, in the world in which we live a major focus has been centered on the subject of national security. For Americans, this subject has become a collective concern due to the events surrounding 9-11. Few argue this point; however, the particular strategies, whether in the form of enhanced border security, the Patriot Act, or the War in Iraq, have been diverse and resulted in contentious reaction.

As important to this ongoing debate as the physical actions taken, is the mindset of the government and the general public regarding national security during the process. It is in this highly dynamic environment that the "Politics of the Playground" is forwarded. Before this concept is advanced it should be noted that the dilemma of national security is truly complex in nature. Acknowledgment of this complexity is a salient beginning point for not only critiquing the struggles of the current administration, but also when reflecting on the actions and inactions of previous administrations when dealing with this subject. It is with the understanding of the complexity of implementing national security that the general public can judge past, current, and future administrations fairly as well as decide where public support should be given.

A second important point that should be stressed is that giving credence to the complex nature of national security does not require eliminating the implementation of practical strategies, or the usage of common sense. It is within the arena of what is the proper "mindset" for engaging in national security activities that has become the most bitterly fought battleground to date. Conservatives have been attacked for having an overly simplistic mindset on national security. The most salient example of this belief is found in the constant liberal media attack on President Bush. President Bush has been stereotyped as not only simplistic in his actions on national security, but worse yet, dangerous to the future of the country with his straightforward approach to dealing with terrorist threats.

It is interesting to note that while the President has been repeatedly lambasted as incompetent, his straightforward non-nuanced approach has been embraced by the majority of Americans during extremely tenuous times. Recently, this identification with the George Bush philosophy has seen a rollercoaster ride of peaks and valleys in popular support. Many explain the current low poll numbers as the President's strategy of avoiding an aggressive rebuttal of the liberal media's onslaught of his character and competence on most occasions.

In reality, current concerns over the President's ability to properly prosecute national security matters reflect uncertainty within the conservative populace that encompasses a much greater proportion of the nation than is ever reported. It is in reminding conservative minded individuals why the Bush no-nonsense approach to national security rings true to the hearts of most

Americans that the door is opened for the analogy of the "Politics of the Playground."

This analogy should in no way be considered a shortcut to thinking. On the contrary, in the same vein as the President has injected the usage of common sense into a difficult endeavor, the "Politics of the Playground" offers an easily identifiable concept that is applicable to the complex issues we face today.

To enter this realm, one must first take a mental journey back to the elementary school playground. This mental journey differs for every reader for many factors, but once there, we find that we all share many of the same memories that are very applicable to life today. With that image focused in your mind we dissect the impacts of the "playground" then and its modern day relevance to issues such as national security.

For most, the "playground" took on an almost magical aura as a place where several hours of what might be considered compulsory study were released in a 30 minute exultation of freedom. To the mind of the eager student, this was freedom from the rigors of class work as there were no "spelling bees" or "math quizzes" on the playground. In reality, and totally unknown to the student experiencing playground "bliss," the recess period served as much as the testing grounds for classroom knowledge as it did a refreshing period.

For our purposes, the "playground" takes on a deeper meaning in the form of transactions found in daily life. This analogy of the playground as daily life is applicable when identifying the participants at the micro-level (as individuals) or at the macro-level (as countries). For our purposes, we will use our understanding of how we, as individuals, acted and reacted on the playground of life to take us to the macro-level were the same analogy can be applied to the U.S. as a whole.

First, the playground is an arena of laws, contracts, and negotiations. This is seen in the selection of members for group activities such as kickball or baseball. If you recall, these negotiations were often highly contentious, as everyone wanted to win the contest of the day. On the playground, laws came in the form of rules that applied for all members and everyone was obligated to follow the rules of every game. Violators of rules were seldom tolerated by team members, as it threatened the validity of the game. That is to say, high priority was given to following the laws as if every baseball game was the World Series and every football game was the Super Bowl on the playground.

This mentality is reflected at the governmental level of the U.S. today. The U.S. currently enters into contracts with multiple global partners and violations of contracts are expected to bring repercussions. Recently, within the context of national security, this logical (playground) reaction has been drawn into question by liberals. One example is the 17 resolution violations by Saddam Hussein preceding the war in Iraq. Liberals have attacked the administration for enforcing the repercussions clearly stated within U.N. resolutions. Violators on the "playground" eventually found themselves out of the game. Saddam Hussein now finds himself in the same predicament.

The "Politics of the Playground" also incorporates the modern media. Today the media can be most adequately identified as the playground "tattler." As with the media, the tattler was an endless source of information. While the class tattler disseminated information in all forums (playground, classroom, lunchroom, bathroom, etc), the playground was the most fertile ground for information collection.

When reflecting back to the playground, as with today, the tattler sometimes related helpful information. Simple examples would include who was sick, who was in trouble, what was for lunch, and so on. The tattler was all too eager to educate students on the events of the day. However, at times, more often than not, the tattler served as a tool of mis-information and the creator of turmoil. When dealing with destructive forces, such as the playground bully, the tattler could cause much unneeded calamity.

No analogy of the playground would be complete without examining the "bully." Unfortunately, a recollection of the playground bully is all too easy to mentally formulate because of the negative impact this individual(s) had on the playground dynamics. First, a quick reflection on some of the characteristics of the playground bully. What is sometimes forgotten is that the playground bully was not always the physically biggest kid. However, the bully was always the most aggressive and most unpredictable. A constant element of danger fell upon everyone within grasping distance of the bully.

Liberals often take the stance that the U.S. is the bully, and by default deserves the assaults that have befallen the country. This is often articulated indirectly by the stress given to trying to understand those who are attempting to destroy the country over practical survival strategies. Today, the bullies in the world playground are radical Islamic extremists. As with the playground bully, radical Islamists follow an irrational philosophy that is destructive in all forms.

Another aspect of the bully is that he or she often had lackeys in tow. However, the followers of the bully never received equal status and were often punished arbitrarily along with other playground members. In short, safety was never assured in the bully's camp, at best it was delayed. On the world playground, Spain has attempted to find grace with Islamic radicals, if not the liberal factions within its own country, by pulling out of Iraq. Israel has followed suit in its withdrawal from the Gaza Strip in the hopes of finding (bully) peace. The most salient example may be that of France. France, in recent days, has shown itself all too willing to breach its alliances with the U.S. and coalition forces in the War on Terror. Yet, despite these actions, France finds itself battling radical Islamic upheavals within its own country.

Simply put, capitulation to the bully has not excluded France from victimization. Examples throughout history are abundant of attempts to appease the bully. They equal a lengthy historical list of absolute failures. Recall the playground, how many accounts do you have of the bully making peace and playing amicably alongside everyone else? That's right, the bully was always the bully. This point is often exacerbated by the element of the tattler (media). We see a common sense tactic of the Bush administration to often avoid the media. While this tactic can be debated, it follows a general logic incorporated by all students on the playground. On the playground, often one eye is kept on the bully while the other eye is on the tattler. Unfortunately, many times it appears that these two players appear to blur in identification.

Of course, everyone tries to avoid the bully. The question is what to do when that fails? One option to acquiring safety, and hence normality to the playground, is seeking help from the "teacher/recess monitor." This individual can be equated with the United Nations. As with the United Nations, the teacher's function on the playground, in theory, is to maintain fairness and stability. While often wrapped in good intentions, everyone quickly learns that the teacher is completely ineffective in policing a bully. As soon as the caring eyes of the teacher stray, the bully strikes, and strikes again. Security, in all categories of playground life as in real life, including the following comparisons: recess activities (economics), personal space (border security), personal safety (national security), come about through coalitions of allies, and inevitably through individual action.

It is truly hoped that your memory of the playground bully comes from the recollection of observer and not victim. If you saw these playground abuses from the vantage point of observer you can recall feeling lucky that the bully had not picked you as one of his or her "favorites." If you came out unscathed, luck may have been a factor because the bully is well known for spreading misery.

For the U.S. on the world playground, anonymity is not an option. In many ways, the U.S. in recent history (1990s) has taken repeated beatings despite being the largest kid on the playground. When the bully terrorizes the "big kid" at recess, it is disheartening to everyone. This was because the victim had the capacity to stop the threat but chose not to (on the playground, this is usually because of fear).

For the U.S., this has come about due to the emasculating effects of liberalism. Secondly, it was disheartening because it reinforced the futility of future resistance by others. Currently, under President Bush, the country is showing an attitude of the kid who has decided enough is enough and began to swing. It is these embedded ideals that draw people to the Bush common sense approach to national security. These ideals are unshakable to most Americans as they have been reinforced since the days of the playground.

It is the brilliance, and not the limitation, of the conservative ideology that allows the implementation of common sense approaches as seen in the "Politics of the Playground" into the complex arena of national security. The saving grace for all of us is that the bell has not rung, school is not out, and the chance for additional learning is still attainable. This is fortunate as the U.S. faces a formidable bully with more than a few lackeys in tow. (Ibbetson, 2006, April 4)

In *The Politics of the Playground,* I make the argument that there are some simple truths when it comes to fighting radical Islamic terrorism. Fight or die. However, strangely enough in the political realm, this is not seen as a no brainer but as a highly debatable point of contention. Specifically, liberals constantly beat the drum that the War on Terror is an overreaction which does more bad than good for this country. Surely you have all heard the argument that the battles in the War on Terror, such as that of our military operations in Iraq, have no real link to Osama bin Laden or al Qaeda and are not a proper reaction to the events of 9-11. These are frustrating sentiments indeed as they show, at best, the limits of the liberal vision of a multi-faceted global war as well as the inability of Democrats and their far left base to "straight talk" with the public of their personal weaknesses when it comes to defending this country.

In an unbelievable twist of fate, Democrats have spent as much time attacking the military troops as they have attacking Republicans. You might wonder why someone would attack the military that is simply following orders. You might also wonder how undermining the troops who protect our freedom would be in our best interest. The answer is that it is not in our best interest and it is, at best, a loathsome activity and, at worst, treasonous. While most people can see this activity as wrong, it is valuable to delve deep into these questions as they lead us to the heart of politics today and to the "hearts" of the politicians themselves.

Democrats have found themselves in the terrible position of endorsing failure as their political platform. To a degree, the party not in power always adopts a "change" platform of sorts to compel the voting majority to vote in a different way from the past election. The problem in this situation is that we are at war and Democrats have framed the war discussion in a way that only economic collapse and failure will validate their argument to the American people for the need for an administrational change. This is by no means the only position that Democrats could have championed, but this is the reality which brings me to my second point. With the growing base of the Democratic Party now belonging to the radical left, the party now shares an anti-American, anti-capitalism, socialistic philosophy. This socialistic philosophy embraces the dark view of America in which liberals see the country as "bad" and in need of self punishment, defeat, and total transformation under a Marxian philosophy.

How do you take down a country? First and foremost, you undermine the military forces that protect the economic and civil liberties of the nation. You may be thinking, "Paul, you're not saying that elected officers of the Democratic Party are purposely and unfairly attacking our military fighting forces for political gain?" That is exactly what I am saying. Here's the proof, and it is painful straight talk if you love the military forces as much as I do. As reported by WorldNetDaily.com, John Kerry (D-Ma) told CBS's Bob Schieffer of "Face the Nation" that the terrorizing of Iraqi children by U.S. soldiers needed to stop (WoldNetDaily, 2005). Specifically, WorldNetDaily reported that Kerry said, 'And there is no reason, Bob, that young American soldiers need to be going into the homes of Iraqis in the dead of night, terrorizing kids and children, you know, women...' (WorldNetDaily, p.1, 2005). These statements by Senator John Kerry were totally irresponsible and, in most likelihood, speak to his failure to be seen as being of Presidential timber, but as with Democrats and their opposition to the fundamental principles of conservatism, there is much more and much worse to come.

John Murtha (D-Pa) would openly and publicly condemn marines involved in a shooting incident in Haditha Iraq of being murderers (Burtis, 2006). These condemnations publicly made by Murtha that the Marines were war criminals were made prior to any charges and trial taking place (White, 2006). Murtha was reported to have told reporters that the Marine squad had cracked under the stress of a fallen comrade and 'killed innocent civilians in cold blood' (White, 2006). In a response to Murtha's public pre-trial condemnations, Marine Corps Staff Sergeant Frank D. Wuterich sued for defamation. Neal A. Puckett and Mark S. Zaid would also forward lawsuits against the congressman from Pennsylvania for libel and invasion of privacy saying that Murtha's smear campaign was conducted outside the bounds of his official scope as a congressman (White, 2006). Richard J. Durbin (D-Ill) and Democratic Whip equated the treatment of detainees by military soldiers at Guantanamo Bay, Cuba, with the Nazis, the Soviets, and Pol Pot (Liss, 2005). Under heavy public outcry, Durbin made a public tearful apology of his disparaging statement about the military (Liss, 2005).

Encompassing all the military fighting forces in an act nothing short of treason, Senate Majority Leader Harry Reid, from the floor of the Senate, stated that the war on Iraq was lost (Babbin, 2007). Statements like these absolutely shatter the weak public front forwarded by liberals that 'we support the troops, not the mission.' In a war that has seen such an overt Democratic effort to undermine the military forces in the field of battle, General David Petraeus, a 35-year decorated veteran, would enter the scene to deliver the current Iraq assessment. As with the Murtha debacle, condemnation would be heaped upon Petraeus by a *New York Times* ad reading "General Petraeus or General Betray us?" (Hegseth, 2007). The radical anti-war *MoveOn.org* was reported to have had a close working relationship with congressional Democrats and, at least one Democratic statement implying questions about honesty and the upcoming Petraeus report, had already been collected in the news service *Politico* (Hegseth, 2007).

I think the evidence is more than ample that there is a collective effort by liberal Democrats to undermine the War on Terror and the military has been the undeserving victim. It is important that we think about what is going on in this fight, who's with us and who is against victory, and even how to assess where improvements can be made to ensure a future victory.

The article *Fish Stories* is an attempt to find a balance of straight talk and straight thought in a time of war. I again use an analogy I hope most readers can relate to, the good old fishing trip. War and fishing, hmm, who would have thought a person could put those two together?

Fish Stories: Changing the Way We Talk About the War on Terror

I am a fisherman. I guess you could say that I was bitten by the "fishing bug" as a child and it never let go. If this has happened to you then you know that each year fishermen around the country get that special calling, almost like an internal instinct that kicks in, to break out the tackle box and head to that special lake, pond, or river. For me, I'm called to the ponds of Kansas, locations which I will never disclose, where the bass are dark green, large, and feisty. I'm called to the water each year when the world starts turning green, you know, when the smell of cut grass hits your nose and the crickets and cicadas start playing their evening serenade. While my line seems to hit the water less and less each season, the undeniable yearly urge never diminishes.

One thing I learned early in my fishing career was the existence of the fish story. The fish story is created and continues to exist in any place where at least one lure is sold and two people meet. There are endless variations to the fish story but they often contain common elements which include the following: the perfect day, the perfect lure, the perfect placement, the perfect strike, the perfect fight, and the perfect landing of a lunker.

Let me say from the beginning that the fish story is not a lie, not exactly. The fish story is more accurately described as a glorified version of the truth. That is, there is most often not only an embellishment of the facts, but also an omission of certain details that make the story less appealing. For example, often it's omitted that the perfect weather conditions for fishing only started after three hours of standing in the rain. The use of the perfect lure may exclude the fact that it was only tried after half the lures in the tackle box were on the bottom of the pond or permanent Christmas ornaments in nearby trees. One of the worst things about the fish story is that it can never be repeated in practice; however, the sad thing is that we all try. Everybody wants the grand results as told in the fish story but we forget that we are following a very imperfect accounting of the facts. In the end, trying to emulate the fish story leaves most mosquito bitten, baitless, and angry.

There is obviously a world of difference between fishing and the War on Terror; however, they both share one thing in common, an abundance of fish stories. These stories are created and reproduced by both the left and the right and all are counterproductive to the war effort. On the right, there is a tendency at times to avoid fully disclosing that the War on Terror suffers from what all wars do, and that is an abundance of mistakes. More boots on the ground from the conflict's start probably would have been a better strategy. Not allowing the huge amount of post-conflict looting and infrastructure damage is but one more example of changes that would have probably been implemented if we could do things all over again. I'm not saying that there should be a daily self-chastising by the government, but when the running account of the war purposely avoids the downsides to what is happening, you're hearing a fish story.

While the right should be wary against creating fish stories, the left should be warned against demanding that the country live and conduct war in one. The left is notorious for demanding that every aspect of the war run within the perfect environment of the fish story or it's time to get out! Meanwhile the actual fish story that the left constructs, and wishes the country to follow, is created not in an idyllic vision of how we win, but how we must inevitably lose. One of the fish stories that the left loves, which has to be seen as one of the "whoppers" surrounding the War on Terror, are the various yarns that entail the line of thinking that if we just run from our enemies, they surely will not follow.

When we cut through the embellishments and the omissions, we are left with several facts that seem very different from the standard fish stories told by many on both the left and right. They include the following:

1. Mistakes have been, and will continue to be made in this war. To assume that a level of perfection will at some point be achieved is simply a fish story.
2. The U.S. military is a noble force that remains so even when a handful in the ranks fall from grace.
3. The war in Iraq is a worthy effort that serves the interest of American security as well as the furtherance of democracy.
4. It's a war we can win or lose.
5. For the war in Iraq to be successful, the Iraqis must step forward and defend their right to be free. We cannot do that for them.
6. Until the war in Iraq, and for that matter the War on Terror is over, America will always be at its strongest when united in a common cause. Anyone who tells you that the caustic division over how to protect the nation is a positive thing is telling you the darkest of fish stories.

I sigh at times myself, along with a nation that is becoming war weary. It would be inaccurate to say that the country is weary of the need to secure the nation, but more weary of the loss of American soldiers that the television documents on a daily basis. Weary of a loss of normalcy that war brings to daily life. Most notably, Americans are weary of a lack of victory in this conflict. The concept of stalemates, deadlocks, and quagmires run completely counter to the American psyche. In short, America is a land of winners; anything short of victory is defeat. I feel that the U.S. is at a crossroads in the War on Terror. We will either reach down deep and get our second wind to continue what we started, or we will, in fishing terms, "cut bait." I think that victory in Iraq is far too important for a wavering American resolve to be the factor that causes success in this highly volatile part of the world to be "the one that got away." If Iraq is to become a free nation, a trophy on the mantle of democracy, it will be in part because the American people had the grit to weather the storms of doubt and despair that war always brings. The least any of us can do is speak the unvarnished truth about the challenge. The country would do well to have the fish stories end at the water's edge. (Ibbetson, 2006, August 25)

If we embrace straight talk and straight thought then we have to face the responsibilities of not only our dialogue and actions, but also our feelings. That's right, a conservative talking about feelings. As a human I am a big advocate of feelings and I have them quite often. The events of 9-11 evoked many strong feelings and one of them was anger. I now forward some straight talk about where I believe anger plays a positive role in securing the freedoms and the future of this country. Of course, I won the "Nazi award" from liberals around the country who read this highly circulated article. In actuality, liberals are much angrier than me but with a different type of anger.

The Value of Anger

We have always been taught that anger is a bad thing that should be hidden, suppressed, bottled up, and generally denied expression by any means necessary. To mention the possibility that there may be a time and place where anger may be of value, if not of necessity, is to place oneself in direct jeopardy of being labeled a "hate monger" or something worse. However, I believe there is a very distinct delineation of the displays of anger that may change the minds of some on this contentious emotion, and none too soon. If we look carefully, we can see there are three forms of anger: directionless anger, negative anger, and righteous anger. Bear with me.

First, we observe directionless anger which has been the hallmark of liberals and is aptly displayed in the "Anybody but Bush" emotional tantrums which offer no new ideas, or courses of action, but simply a display of anger for anger's sake. With a possible reprieve coming with the 2008 Presidential election, directionless anger can be seen in those angry souls rigidly hunched behind the wheels of vehicles still displaying those sad little wrinkled and partially bio-degraded "Kerry 2004" bumper stickers. You've seen them, and probably shook your head. Yes, this directionless anger has a very long shelf life and produces nothing.

Second, we can observe the negative anger propagated by radical Islam which fuels the terrorist in a never ending cycle of intolerance to all who do not conform to their belief system. Negative anger feeds and replenishes itself unendingly, and the exaltation we see for the killing of innocent men, women, and children is but a mere taste of its potential destructive capability.

Third, and I am afraid to admit maybe the most unpopular anger in America, is that of righteous anger. This is the anger felt by those who see the blessings of this nation, the blessings bestowed upon this country by God, being taken away. This righteous anger was displayed by none other than Jesus Christ when he saw the desecration of the holy temple by the merchants. In a righteous anger, Jesus ejected the merchants by force from the temple and thereby restored the holy place as God had intended it to be. There is little doubt that Christians are given great guidance and restraint on the usage of anger within the Bible. However, as importantly, the Bible explains that as children of God, the emotions we have, including anger, are a part of the miracle of our creation.

It is not the validity of the emotion of anger that should be in question, but to what ends we use this emotion. When I think about the innocence of life so unjustifiably taken during 9-11, when I watch our elected officials waiver on the simple construction of a border fence, or observe citizens like the Minutemen being harassed and besmirched for attempting to protect a border our government has abandoned, a strong emotion builds within me. That emotion is anger. How about you? Liberals would have you replace this righteous anger with apathy, an apathy that is based on the idea that America is evil and deserves its punishment and, of course, that no defense, whether a border barrier or otherwise, can actually work. I reject this mentality with every fiber of my being and submit that a healthy dose of anger may be just what is needed if we are to collectively get off our duffs and compel our government officials to protect and thereby save this country. I think that right after 9-11, for a brief moment, together we were angry. For a moment, we as a country identified an unholy force that was bent to destroy the most blessed country in the world, and we were angry, we were united, and we were a force to be reckoned with.

In closing, I would say that we must look to God for guidance in these turbulent times as did our founding fathers. We should allow his spirit to guide us and direct us in the challenges ahead. As we do this we should remember that anger is one of the gifts of our creation, not a mistake or an abomination. Maybe, just maybe, as the country crumbles piece by piece under the attack of radical Islam, with the assistance of an apathetic border security policy, we should entertain the possibility of collectively getting a little angrier while we still can. (Ibbetson, 2007, July 7)

References

Babbin, J. (2007, April 20). Harry Reid, loser. *Human Events.com*. Retrieved December 23, 2007, from http://www.humanevents.com/article.php?id=20347

Burtis, J. (2006, June 2). John Murtha-first the guilty verdict, then the trial. *Canada Free Press*. Retrieved December 23, 2007, from http://www.canadafreepress.com/2006/burtis060206.htm

Hegseth, P. (2007, September 9). MoveOn.org calls Petraeus a traitor. *The Weekly Standard*. Retrieved December 23, 2007, from http://www.weeklystandard.com/Content/Public/Articles/000/000/014/091rhesh.asp

Ibbetson, P. A. (2006, April 4). The politics of the playground. *News By Us*. Retrieved from http://newsbyus.com/more.php?id=A2832_0_1_0_M

Ibbetson, P. A. (2006, August 25). Fish stories: Changing the way we talk about the war on terror. *Canada Free Press*. Retrieved from http://www.canadafreepress.com/2006/ibbetson082506.htm

Ibbetson, P. A. (2007, July 7). The Value of Anger. *Capitol Hill Coffee House*. Retrieved from http://capitolhillcoffeehouse.com/more.php?id=3559_0_1_0_M

Liss, K. (2005, June 22). Durbin apologizes for Nazi, Gulag, Pol Pot remarks. *Fox News.com*. Retrieved December 23, 2007, from http://www.foxnews.com/story/0,2933,160275,00.html

Murray, S. (2005, June 22). Durbin apologizes for remarks on abuse [Electronic version]. *Washington Post*, p.A06. Retrieved January, 5, 2008, from http://www.washingtonpost.com/wp-dyn/content/article/2005/06/21/AR2005062101654.html

White, J. (2006, August 2). Haditha Marine sues John Murtha for defamation. *Washington Post,* A05. Retrieved December 23, 2007, from http://sweetness-light.com/archive/marine-sues-murtha-for-defamation

WorldNetDaily.com. (2005, December 6). Kerry: 'U.S. soldiers terrorize kids.' *World Net Daily.* Retrieved December 23, 2007, from http://www.worldnetdaily.com/news/article.asp?ARTICLE_ID=47765

Here are some of the angry chalk writings from liberals at Kansas State University when Rush Limbaugh funnyman, Paul Shanklin, was preparing to be a guest on the Conscience of Kansas radio program. I told him about the writings and Shanklin addressed the Kansas State Young Democrats using his impersonation skills as Barack Obama. I laughed until it hurt.

My story for this book begins and ends right here at Kansas State University.

The statue of Johnny Kaw, the Kansas version of Paul Bunyan that I played on when I was a child still stands today in Manhattan, Kansas.

A little look inside the radio station at KSDB Manhattan 91.9 f.m.

Here is a picture of the award I received from the Kansas Association of Broadcasters for best graduate radio program for 2008 for the 'Conscience of Kansas.'

Here is a picture of our beautiful bay window at the radio station. Sometimes liberals come by and make faces during the show. I wonder if they know that we video tape all the shows and I make fun of them on air and then put it all on YouTube.

Here I am listening intently to a liberal caller explain why Barack Obama will make the world a better place as President.

Laying down the law on the Conscience of Kansas radio show.

Here I am preparing for my radio interview with Duane 'Dog' Chapman on the Conscience of Kansas radio program.

Displaying my letter from President George W. Bush on my first book 'Living Under The Patriot Act: Educating A Society.'

Chapter 5

Polar Bears and Ice Cubes

IN THE ZOO WE SEE the appearance of normalcy that we look for and expect in real life. What I mean is that the penguins have cute little slipper slides that end in temperature controlled water. The polar bears have their own controlled environment that mimics our perception of what their ideal habitat should be and hefty amounts of fish are laid out promptly at 9:00 a.m. as it should be in a properly organized world. The thing is we, as humans, like order almost as much as we like control. At the zoo, each strategically placed bamboo tree, cave, feeder, and lily pad are visual illustrations of our ability to create an environment in a way we think it should look. We try our best to make animals feel like they are in their natural habitats. However, from time to time we are forced to face the fact that we just don't know as much about nature as we think we do. That is, we are an intelligent bunch of humans, but smarts alone can't always keep the crocodiles happy and it certainly won't make the pandas mate. While that's just a couple of small problems at the zoo, some worry about what to do with the entire planet.

I laugh when I hear questions about what we should do about the planet tossed about as it implies to me there is a feeling of cosmic superiority by some when this subject is broached, especially in the case of global warming. Let me get it out there from the beginning that I am not against global conservation. I believe that we should all be good stewards of the planet but, differing from liberals, I see it as a personal responsibility and not a place for government mandates. Any time the government mandates a program, it is a direct reflection of a belief that individuals will not do the function of the said program on their own, or do it properly. It is also a direct shortcut around observing free market principles, people's ability to be charitable, responsible, and just plain free thinking. When it comes to issues like global warming, major economically crippling initiatives are brought to the table by activist zealots with no more evidence of the need for their initiatives than a fear for polar bears and ice cubes. I use the analogy of polar bears because it is a scene framed by liberal environmentalists in the manmade global warming argument of an impending extinction of the white giants that is repeated everywhere when there is no definitive proof that this is the case. In fact, it's a lie. To date, the hunting of polar bears has much more viability as a threat than global warming. However, hunting does not fit the current narrative of doom being spun by the global warming community. The continental ice shelf may indeed be melting, but its relationship to manmade activity is absolutely not clear, nor is our certain demise as a species imminent from such a reduction of the continental ice shelf. This is neither brain surgery nor rocket science, it is simply a historical fact that the planet has and continues to warm and cool, as well as go into and out of ice ages. What I am concerned about is the loss of a bunch of mighty fine ice cubes! Beverage lovers beware!

The global warming fad is packaged in a sterling case of scientific superiority. We are more than encouraged to jump aboard this ship of fools while fruitcakes like Al Gore wave to us from the captain's chair. Did I mention that I do not endorse the idea of manmade global warming? These fanatics have all but abandoned any acknowledgment of the cyclical nature of global warming. Yes, to the fear mongers like Al Gore and company, it's all man, and if we are really going do some straight talking, it's all the United States' fault. It makes sense for the global warming doomsayers, with their underlying socialist movement, to reject natural forces as an influence since you can't very well place a government sanction on, for instance, the volcano at Krakatau or a fissure at the bottom of the ocean.

In the absence of observing natural phenomena which I believe account for most, if not all, of the climate change that is occurring, liberals wish to use a socialistic form of government to mandate the heck out of flocculent cows, hairspray, and, of course, your evil SUV. Lastly, the global warming community demands that citizens endorse the idea that the scientific community can gauge the weather with unquestioned accuracy ten years in the future when the weatherman can't get the weather right for the end of the week. Am I right or am I right? However, from the standpoint of those who want to tear down this country and take away your constitutional rights, in my estimation there is a practical reason for this strategy. That is, by placing the catastrophe of global warming a decade or so in the future, global warmer proponents feel less pressure to explain natural weather phenomena that may take place in the present that directly contradicts their doomsday theory. We just have to believe that everything will make sense sometime down the road. This is nonsense.

My global warming articles have been the most widely read of all my articles to date. When I joined the global warming debate I did so out of exasperation. With issues such as American hostages being taken captive by terrorists and having their heads removed on video, the priority of polar bears and ice cubes should not have been called into question. With Al Gore firmly placing global warming as a greater threat than terrorism, I thought I would try to create a respectful discussion, well, as respectful as I can make it on the topic, in hopes that people would not fall too far down the rabbit hole of insanity. In my own humble way, I thought titling my article: *Can Global Warming Cut Your Head Off?*, would get to the point and avoid any ambiguity about how I felt about the importance of manmade global warming versus the War on Terror. What I opened up was a fire storm. An environmental jihad, if you will, was unleashed upon me in a way that I never expected. I leave it to the reader to decide if I was over the line or off base with my article. After you, the reader, have read the article, I will explain how some people responded and what I did about it.

Can Global Warming Cut Your Head Off?

Can global warming cut your head off? Well can it? I know, that's a silly question but welcome to the wacky world of crazy statements that make up the arena of the global warming scaremongers. Currently, the Mayor of Crazy Town is Al Gore. Al Gore has always been in search of a wedge issue to divide the American people and push additional power to the government. In today's world, the global warming agenda has become an interesting tool for advancing socialism. First, if I can get through the underlying premise of global warming without falling out of my chair, here is what the uneducated person is supposed to take away from the global warming sales pitch.

1. There is absolutely no doubt that manmade global warming is happening.
2. Every person of high qualification agrees on this issue and to question the existence of global warming is to commit an act of lone stupidity.
3. You, as a member of society, caused global warming by your negligence.
4. You, as the guilty party, must now make penance for your actions by following a modification program created by those smarter and obviously more humane than you (Big Government).

If you visit Al Gore's movie promo website for his upcoming film, *An Inconvenient Truth*, they will hit you with these statements that verify my previous assertions. Here is a quote from the website: 'The vast majority of scientists agree that global warming is real, it's already happening and that it is the result of our activities and not a natural occurrence. The evidence is overwhelming and undeniable' (http://www.climatecrisis.net/thescience/).

What always follows in the guilt trip phase of the global warming sales pitch is the lengthy list of terrible catastrophes that will befall the planet, "remember this is all because of you," in the near future without radical changes in the way people live their lives. According to Al Gore and company, the list of impending doom brought forth by global warming includes, but is not limited to, future deaths from global warming to reach 300,000 yearly in 25 years and the absence of a single ice cube in the Artic Ocean by the year 2050 (http://www.climatecrisis.net/thescience/). In fact, if you hunt hard enough in the global warming literature, you can see global warming as the suspected culprit for most of the problems in the world.

My complaint with the global warming community goes beyond the fact that most global warming proponents embrace Gore's website wording that global warming is a genuinely agreed upon fact when in reality it is highly debated. The global warming school of scare tactics was born out of the failed school of global cooling that was just as vehemently preached in the 1970s. Just as sure as the global coolies were that the world was doomed to an inevitable freeze-over, the global warmest of today fails to ponder alternative theories such as the cyclic nature of weather patterns and so forth. I have to admit that this is frustrating to me; however, as a compassionate conservative I restrain my wrath for extremists like Gore until his warped sense of reality starts to undermine the national security of the country. That is, when the man who almost became President of the United States says that global warming is more dangerous to the country than international terrorism, I have to stand up and say, "Wait a minute!"

I would simply forward the following questions to all those who think that Gore is still hitting on all his cylinders after he and others promote global warming over terrorism as our top threat today. Since September 11, 2001, have we had 5,042 attacks of global warming? We have from terrorism (thereligionofpeace.com). Has global warming sent any videotapes lately that speak of our ultimate destruction as a country? I am still checking the records for an official fatwa sent by global warming on the U.S. There must be one for brain children such as Al Gore to assert to the public that they should, after weighing both issues, decide that terrorism be placed on the back burner to global warming. Al Gore must be privy to some special information that is restricted from the public? I mean, this is the only conceivable answer that would allow a man who was Vice President of the United States, and in the inner loop for terrorist information, to perceive that the global Islamic mandate by Osama bin Laden for all Muslims to kill every American they have contact with is less pressing than issues such as the rain forest. Surely a grand Gorian movement to focus the masses on global warming would also work hand in hand with that little secondary threat of terrorism. Right? I can only assume that our future hybrid cars will give us at least some protection from a dirty bomb explosion. Possibly the newest series of windmill systems will be able to detect at least a small amount of terrorist communications? I know, this is as silly as Gore is crazy, but this is the common dialogue in Crazy Town where the most obvious things must be pushed directly in front of the face of the wacko environmentalists for reality to sink in. So I ask you, can global warming cut your head off? Maybe make a video of the event to send to your family? It's time to separate the silly from the dangerous on this issue.

I am dubious of the viability of manmade global warming in general due to a lack of substantial hard scientific evidence for its existence. I oppose the underlying socialistic agenda that is forwarded under the guise of global warming. I charge those, such as Al Gore, who would shift our focus from the defense of the nation in time of war as being dangerously misguided. The Gore philosophy of de-emphasizing the threat of terrorism helps the terrorist cause. I challenge anyone to make a cogent argument that 10 years of unbridled terrorism will have less impact on the U.S. than 10 years of Americans driving SUV's by herds of flocculent cattle on their way to charcoal burning barbeques. America cannot afford to be lulled into a false sense of security, or dragged onto false battlegrounds. The radical Islamic terrorists of today would, if allowed, lay waste to all America in a moment. So as Al Gore seeks your signed pledge on his promo website to watch his movie, I would ask you to at least take a moment to remember the thousands of Americans who have, and continue, to die in this little secondary problem the country faces called the War on Terror. That is, if it's not too inconvenient? (Ibbetson, 2006, June 3)

The first thing I noticed a few weeks after publishing this article was that it was being republished all over the world. Both environmental websites as well as global warming skeptics literally ate the article up. I was deluged by letters to the editors with no one taking anything but a strong stance for or against my ideas. After writing on some other topics of interest, I decided to look even closer into Al Gore's *Inconvenient Truth* which had been released since the time of the first article. With the publishing of my second article on global warming, *Behind the Curtain: Revisiting Global Warming and the War on Terror,* I hit the liberal environmentalists where they live; that is, I took on their rising star, Al Gore, and exposed him as a fraud while injecting a little bit of good old fashioned humor along the way. Wow, did the liberals get mad. I now had crazy environmentalist groupies like Kevin Grandia in Canada from desmogblog.com, and mindless lackeys of the environmentalist establishment throwing venom my way. In their critiques, my article would be condemned over a question of what year a survey used in the article was released and that some detractors did not like my choice of survey questions I used to support my article. The fervor involved in the attack on the article made it only too obvious that I had struck a nerve.

Yes, I created hordes of allies and enemies on both sides of the issue from the article. The letters to the editor tripled. To the global warmers, I had officially made the villains list and, thanks to transcription software, I now could receive hate mail in six different languages. Believe me, you have not lived until you've been cursed out in French.

One of the factors I believe really angered the left in this article was my ability to show how apocalyptical scenarios can easily fit into just about any fear campaign. I later learned that people would often get a kick out of reading my hate mail, as well as getting an interesting insight into the angry minds of liberals. I now try to save all my "love" and "hate" mail for public viewing at http://www.ibbetsonusa.com. Some of our reader letters will be included in the back of the book for your amusement and to recognize some of the fine websites that publish my articles. If you want a good laugh, read mail from a liberal when they are mad and their fingers are smashing those computer keys.

Behind the Curtain: Revisiting Global Warming and the War on Terror

I recently wrote an article entitled *Can Global Warming Cut Your Head Off ?*, in which I looked at Al Gore's apocalyptic theatrical release of *An Inconvenient Truth*. The focus of my article was to highlight the immediate dangers faced by the country from terrorism in contrast to the highly controversial and ever changing opinions on whether global warming exists, and if so, is it a manmade phenomena? First, I would like to thank all the readers from around the world who read the article. The input I received was overwhelming in the form of both those who agreed with my assertions as well as the many who dug deep in their dictionaries for creative ways to show their disapproval. In the end, it seemed that a revisiting of the subject was necessary. Before I do that, let me forward some of the newest information on this catastrophe we call global warming. In a recent article, the following warnings are forwarded:

'There are ominous signs that the Earth's weather patterns have begun to change dramatically and that these changes may portend a drastic decline in food production -- with serious political implications for just about every nation on Earth. The drop in food output could begin quite soon, perhaps only 10 years from now…The evidence in support of these predictions has now begun to accumulate so massively that meteorologists are hard-pressed to keep up with it…

'During the same time, the average temperature around the equator has risen a fraction of a degree–a fraction that in some areas can mean drought and desolation. Last April, in the most devastating outbreak of tornadoes ever recorded, 148 twisters killed more than 300 people and caused half a billion dollars' worth of damage in 13 U.S. states.'

My friends, while there is much more to this article, at this point I must admit to a little trickery. This article, full of scientific backing which also describes impending doom around the corner for the planet is real; however, it was written in Newsweek on April 28, 1975, by Peter Gwynne and entitled, The Cooling World. Yes, this was one of many global scare stories that swept the nation in the 1970s about a fragile planet in crisis. If truth be told, I am sure that many reading the information in this article were shaking their heads in agreement until the point that the deception was made clear. Those readers may be a little upset now and I join them in this anger as no one likes to be tricked. That's the point of this article. The difference between Al Gore and myself is that I will take you backstage, behind the smoke and mirrors, and show you how the tricks of the global warming trade are performed, tricks that are reported as the truth. Be prepared, because it is a different world behind the curtain. As well, I will address how Al Gore's selective science on global warming has become a dangerous diversion from the clear and present danger the U.S. and world faces from international terrorism.

First, let me say that I am no more a scientist than Al Gore. I am a conservative thinker, and being so I am able to separate theory from reality and emotion from fact. This is a very important point as it's often Al Gore's undoing. For the ex-Vice President, it would be nice, in theory, if the entire scientific community agreed with him that global warming was both human induced and catastrophic. It is such a nice thought, and coincidentally a great marketing tool, that he has adopted it as fact and he serves up this illusion to the American people daily. As early as 1992, Gore was touting that 98% of scientists agreed with him on the global warming issue. In reality, a survey of the American Geophysical Union and American Meteorological Society taken in the same year found that only 17% of scientists endorsed the greenhouse gas climate theory (Saunders, 2006). This great disparity between the number of scientists that Al Gore may wish believe in his apocalyptic view of the planet, and more importantly, the number he attempts to sell to the public, have been, and remain, a padded number. Here are a few modern day examples of scientists in the field who break with the great pied piper of doom: Colorado State University hurricane expert William Gray asserts that the earth will begin to cool sometime in the next 10 years, MIT's climate scientist Robert Lindzen believes that cloud and water vapor will counteract greenhouse gas emissions, and the former director of the National Hurricane Center states that the global warming scare is akin to "a hoax" (Saunders, 2006). But, why worry about any number of naysayers when you can just let go and be carried away in the "awe" of the blockbuster global warming experience!

Al Gore presents emotion evoking imagery not seen since the 2004 Hollywood release of The Day After Tomorrow. The ad posters for An Inconvenient Truth show a monstrous hurricane creeping from an industrial smokestack (Tracinski, 2006). These visuals are designed to spark not only the morbid curiosity of potential viewers but, in the end, Gore's carefully crafted theatrical lesson of morality like those taught to viewers in classics such as "Frankenstein." If you remember the old horror film, the story portrayed an uncontrollable manmade monster that roamed the countryside wreaking havoc. Of course, in the global warming scenario, all mankind must take the role of the misguided, if not evil, Dr. Frankenstein. Back in the real world, the scientific community is very divided about global warming and an increase in hurricane activity which begins Al Gore's Hollywood sideshow. As well as the recent Washington Times survey of various top hurricane scientists that were divided on the issue, additional studies assert that when the recent increase in large scale (category 4-5) hurricanes in the Atlantic are balanced against the decrease of the same scale hurricanes in the Pacific, the overall increase is virtually zilch (Tracinski, 2006). If you are starting to lose your fear and self-loathing over global warming, more images of doom quickly fill the void.

One especially unsettling image is a large tanker sitting stranded in an apparent desert in the once Aral Sea. Gore alludes to the fact that global warming has dried this Asian sea that was once the fourth largest in the world. Wow, that's scary! Conveniently, he forgets to tell viewers that three-quarters of the rivers that fed the sea were purposely diverted by the Soviet Union (Ponte & Morano, 2006). You see, like a good magic show, the water really hasn't disappeared; it's just backstage behind the curtain where you can't see it. This same deception is replicated in photos of disappearing snow on an African mountain in which Gore grimly states that within a decade there will be no snow on Mt. Kilimanjaro (Ponte & Morano, 2006). Once again, Gore avoids scientific data that does not endorse his grim view of the state of the planet. Specifically, he omits the 2003 findings by the British science journal Nature that stated that the loss of snow collection on Mt. Kilimanjaro is really the product of deforestation (Ponte & Morano, 2006). These findings were validated in 2004 by the International Journal of Climatology and the Journal of Geophysical Research.

The question is why so much deception? Will there be a disclosure at the end of the show where Gore explains all the tricks to the crowd. There is little doubt that in the realm of the environmental scaremongers, Gore is the Mayor of Crazy Town and he wants to sell you all a little piece of real estate within the city limits. However, the timing of his renewed crusade has further underpinnings that reflect directly on the War on Terror and the state of mind of liberals today. Al Gore is a prime example of a liberal's inability to embrace national defense policy even when the stakes are at their highest. Las Vegas comedian Julia Gorin gets it right when she says 'While the hawks among us worry about preventing the Armageddon that's coming, our modern-day hippies just want to make sure the planet is pristine when it does. In fact, the more menacing terrorism becomes, the more some people seem to worry about the weather' (Gorin, ¶3, 2006). Gorin concludes her thoughts with a question a lot of us ask by saying, 'Why are these people so worried about the environment, anyway? It's not like they're living on this planet' (Gorin, ¶4, 2006).

The problem is that we all, liberal and conservative, stand to suffer dire consequences from a lack of a unified effort to fight the growing threat of terrorism. I would be the last to say that someone should take away Al Gore's right to play weather hawk in a world that cries out for war hawks; however, I am hopeful that people will see behind the smoke and mirrors of An Inconvenient Truth and focus their attention on the survival of this country. Al Gore has given this weak worn-out planet less than 10 years before it is completely terminal (Will, 2005). Very conveniently this would give just enough time for the American people to place Gore into the White House and allow his visionary intellect and magical skill to reverse the sins of man through the power of the presidency. Will we see another Gore ticket for President? It is most certain that he will not conjure up another joint effort with Senator Joe Lieberman. Lieberman, the Senator from Connecticut, is currently a pariah in the Democratic Party for his strong stand on the War on Terror. Sorry Joe, you just don't have the right set of priorities. In the end, the level of public acceptance for Gore's global warming quest may have a direct impact on a potential 2008 Presidential bid. If this turns out to be true, the American people have the unique opportunity to strike two blows for "sanity" in one fell swoop. So, as the enemy's missiles fly near our allies in Japan, and fall on the homes of Israel, I ask you where should our priorities be? As terrorist plots are uncovered on a regular basis on U.S. soil, where will we focus our efforts for the future? Will we unite to fight the immediate threat of terrorism, or shall we allow ourselves to continue to be mesmerized by Al Gore's magic show, when we truly know what is happening behind the curtain. (Ibbetson, 2006, July 27)

Looking back at the fundamentals of conservatism, we can see the conflicts that face the manmade global warming doomsayers with the rest of the country. At its basic core, manmade global warming environmentalists see the world as helpless and man as all powerful. There is no other adequate answer to this question. The infallibility of God to create a planet that his creations, that's us folks, could cohabitate on without destroying is never allowed in the global warming discussion. In fact, the liberal assumption of a lack of a supreme being is evident in the arrogance that global warmers use in placing science as god to prognosticate the future dates that the human race will be beyond the point of no return. What arrogance, what ignorance. After writing two articles on global warming, and almost being fed to the lions myself, I came to the conclusion that the diehard environmentalists and the liberal political operatives, who cloak themselves among the global warming crowd, had surpassed the sphere of environmentalism and had entered into the domain of religion. It is in the realm of religion that the fervor to oppose and destroy those who wish to question manmade global warming takes place.

I would dare to say that after completing my first two articles, that one would receive no harsher an opposition from opening a Playboy magazine in church than to question manmade global warming. In both cases the same defense is being mounted, that is the defense of religion. Of course, the religion of global warming is an unholy religion where man and science have replaced God and now rule the Earth in every facet with a perceived superior knowledge to that of the creator. A part of the divine plan by the prophets of the religion of global warming, such as Al Gore, is the restriction of free will through the usage of socialism. In many ways the same old push but with a different spin. I was more than happy to publish an article to identify this new religion for inspection by readers and it was by far the largest read article of the global warming series. So enjoy the article with its humor definitely at the expense of Al Gore & Co. but remember to keep the laughter down, after all, you are in church.

From the Pew to the Pulpit: Inside the Church of Global Warming

Walk carefully, I say unto you, for thou art on holy ground. This was the rude awakening that I received when I entered the global warming debate. It would also be the warning that I would forward to anyone wishing to enter the debate over the validity of manmade global warming. I stepped into this discussion after watching the similarities between the scare tactics of the global warmers and what I had seen of the scientific community's certainty of global cooling back in the 1970s. When ex-Vice President Al Gore started saying, in a time of war, that global warming was a more important issue for us all to focus upon than international terrorism, I placed even more focus on the issue. With the help of the scientific community, those who have reservations on the magnitude of reported manmade global warming, I wrote two compelling articles meant to spark further debate on where we should prioritize this issue when the nation is at war. I was literally assailed by the fanatics of the global warming community. The Salt Spring News pen pusher wished to enlighten me to the fact that Al Gore must be brilliant because his theatrical release, which I consider to be a movie equivalent to a 5th grade slideshow, *An Inconvenient Truth*, was doing financially well even though it was only being aired in 77 theatres. Much harsher criticism would be thrust upon me by Harvey Leifert, the Public Information Manager for the American Geophysical Union. Leifert would take offense with a cited paper source that came from a survey of the American Geophysical Union. Leifert stated that the selection of the survey question did not reflect a complete picture of their survey. What was interesting to see was the fervor in which the Public Information Manager would condemn a skeptic. Though he completely side-stepped addressing the main argument that I deduced, that Al Gore's movie, *An Inconvenient Truth*, was akin to a low stakes shell game, his rage over the fact that I would challenge manmade global warming literally made spittle fly off his letter to the editor. Within moments, little smoggy bloggers from Canada, whose creed must be 'We don't think for ourselves, we leave that to the professionals,' would jump to the aid of the American Geophysical Union and firmly ensconce me in their 'Halls of Shame.' This anger, which goes beyond the realm of debate, leads me to a new conclusion as to what motivates the majority of the global warming community. What may have started as the observance of science and environmentalism has now progressed to the level of cultish religion.

If this seems like a stretch, take a moment to look at the evidence that is made available daily. Al Gore, a failed presidential candidate, is hailed as a visionary by championing the global warming cause. His slideshow movie, as I affectionately call it, wins an Oscar and the liberal Hollywood elites praise his name, not unlike a modern day savior. CBS's Harry Smith would broach the topic, what global warmers may whisper at the dinner table; which is, of course, that Al Gore may indeed be a modern day prophet (Rule, 2007). Gore's anointing as a holy man would be made complete with a Noble Peace Prize, which looms in the near future. All we have to do is step inside the church of global warming to understand the fanaticism of doomed earth believers. In this scheme, to question any aspect of global warming is not to invite debate, it is to blaspheme. Manmade global warming skeptics are not people with a different view, they are the equivalent of witches and warlocks whose voices must be burned from existence. Am I too harsh in saying this? Likened to a religious edict, Gore has stated that all skeptic debate is to be silenced through the ludicrous announcement of a "scientific consensus" on the issue. Talk about asking the choir to take a leap of faith.

It is within the contradictions of the global warming argument, as well as the banner carriers, that we start to see just how much one must throw logic out the window to support the global warming machine. What do you do when your prophets no longer live up to the image they portray? When they violate the commandments they themselves have laid down? This is something that religious cults have had to try to deal with on many occasions. Jim Jones who preached socialistic holiness, termed "apostolic socialism," was guilty of physically and emotionally abusing both men and women from within his flock. The contradictions of both his actions and his vision of the future would lead his congregation of over 900 faithful to a cult death in Guyana in what Jones would term "revolutionary suicide." The death of the followers of the Peoples Temple, of which Jones was their prophet, should have taught us all the lesson that we must be very careful to never exalt people or ideas to the level of the cult status. Is there no comparison between the Peoples Temple and the Doomsayers of Global Warming?

Al Gore, on a daily basis, requests that all Americans make that walk from the pew to the pulpit, within the church of global warming, to limit their CO2 fossil fuel emissions to save the planet no matter what the personal cost may be. Of course we would expect the portly prophet of doomsday prognostications to be the most pious when it comes to his own CO2 emissions, right? Sorry flock. Gore has been found to be lumbering across the globe with a personal carbon footprint the size of Sasquatch. According to Nashville Electric Service records, Gore's palatial home and pool house use more than twenty times the national average of kilowatt-hours (Tapper, 2007). So what do you do when your leader, who preaches that the masses should reduce their deadly emissions, is found with his pants down consuming enough energy to power a third world country? Well, that's when fanaticism comes in handy. We are quickly told that Gore is still among the holy, despite the fact that his utility bill was $30,000 in a single year. Why? Because he had a coupon! Thus enters the saga of the carbon credit. Like group hypnosis, the carbon credit sales pitch conditions the global warming convert to believe that if you have enough money, your spirit can be pure, without reducing your carbon footprint at all. Of course the ones that do not have the financial means will have to be doing the sacrificing, but by expanding government regulation there is little doubt that a fair and even reduction system can be found for the unwashed masses. In case you don't understand this system, it's called socialism, and it's the business end of the church of global warming. There is little doubt that when we get to this point, we will be asked to put a lot more than money into the collection plate; but for the prophet Gore, this will never be a problem. Even at Global Warming Hearings in the Senate in late March 2007, where the red carpet was laid in his honor, the prophet of consumption reduction refused to take an energy ethics pledge to use no more energy than the average American. If this article is making you rant, I'm going to have to ask you to quiet down; after all, we are in church.

We have seen the same kind of fanaticism in the push for the United States to join the already failing carbon emission program in Kyoto (Murphy, 2007). That's right, even the believers abroad that are free from the taint of individuality that stains the American consciousness seem to be in constant violation of Kyoto carbon emission limits. Canada's emissions are reported to run at 24 percent with their agreed limit set at

6 percent. Japan runs at 13 percent which is 7 percent higher than their target limit. The original members of Kyoto, the Europeans (EU-15), carbon emission has risen for the second year in a row. Of course one of the world's biggest growing polluters, China, is not even a part of the Kyoto agreement; but hey, it's a great place to buy a carbon credit!

In the end, no one is really reducing carbon emissions, but the rhetoric is running full blast. What are the limits to the global warming hoopla? Will we be seeing little smiling people with billboards and bells selling carbon credit coupons at the airports? I want to exhale in exasperation, but to do so is to kill the planet; you know CO_2. In time, the church of global warming will close its doors with its parishioners having exceeded their cool-aid tolerance level. The confusion, if not the deception, that Al Gore and his minions propagate about "who is the creator, and who is the created" will be swept away. I look forward to that time when so many of my brothers and sisters, currently enthralled by the church of global warming, will come home. So many of us look forward to that day, and like with the story of the prodigal son, when they do come home, there will great rejoicing and a wondrous feast. (Ibbetson, 2007, April 13)

References

Gorin, J. (2006, July 14). Global warbling [Electronic version]. *The Christian Science Monitor.* Retrieved July 15, 2006, from http://www.csmonitor.com/2006/0714/p20s01-ussc.htm

Gwynne, P. (1975, April 28). The cooling world. *Newsweek.* Retrieved July 16, 2006, from http://www.denisdutton.com/cooling_world.htm

Ibbetson, P. A. (2006, June 3). Can global warming cut your head off? *Canada Free Press.* Retrieved from http://www.canadafreepress.com/2006/ibbetson060306.htm

Ibbetson, P. A. (2006, July 27). Behind the curtain: Revisiting global warming and the war on terror. *Canada Free Press.* Retrieved from http://www.canadafreepress.com/2006/ibbetson072706.htm

Ibbetson, P. A. (2007, April 13). From the pew to the pulpit: Inside the church of global warming. *Canada Free Press.* Retrieved from http://www.canadafreepress.com/2007/ibbetson041307.htm

Murphy, C. (2007, July 31). The dirty secret behind Kyoto. *CNN Money.com.* Retrieved March 4, 2007, from http://money.cnn.com/2006/07/28/news/international/pluggedin_murphy.fortune/index.htm?cnn=yes

Ponte, L., & Morano, M. (2006, July). Global warming controversy: Legitimate threat or hot air? *NewsMax, 8,* 16-30.

Rule, M. (2007, February 9). CBS's Harry Smith: 'Is Al Gore a prophet?'. *NewsBusters.* Retrieved March 4, 2007, from http://newsbusters.org/node/10726

Saunders, D. (2006, June 13). Global warming fever [Electronic version]. *San Francisco Chronicle,* p. B9. Retrieved July 16, 2006, from

http://www.sfgate.com/cgi-bin/article.cgi?file=/c/a/2006/06/13/
EDGDOILMDO1.DTL&ty

Tapper, J. (2007, February 26). Al Gore's 'inconvenient truth'? -- a
$30,000 utility bill. *ABC News.* Retrieved March 4, 2007, from
http://abcnews.go.com/Politics/print?id=2906888

Tracinski, R. (2006, June 7). Al Gore is a brave truth teller? *Real Clear
Politics.* Retrieved July 12, 2006, from http://www.realclearpolitics.
com/articles/2006/06/the_truth_is_inconvenient.html

Will, G. (2006, June 11). Gore's warming to a candidacy? *Real Clear
Politics.* Retrieved July 15, 2006, from http://www.realclearpolitics.
com/articles/2006/06/gores_warming_to_a_candidacy.html

Chapter 6

For Those Who Would Kill All The Animals

LIKE I'VE SAID BEFORE, LIFE is like a trip to the zoo. This country has tremendous diversity and with it we find that we don't always get along on every issue. Some of the things people in the U.S. do when we don't agree are as strange and bizarre as anything one might see in the zoo. Are there really any arguments here? It's our country, we made it, and regardless of its downfalls it's the greatest in the world. America is the only country on the planet to which people will paddle in trash cans in the ocean to gain admittance. America is the only country to which people will walk across the desert without water to gain admittance. Everybody comes, and nobody wants to leave. With all that said, there are some folks in this world that don't like America's interesting zoo life. Folks, like those who have radicalized the religion of Islam, believe that their mission in life is our utter destruction.

September 11, 2001, was the biggest success of terrorism against America to date. The battle had been waging for years prior and our inability to recognize, or lack of fortitude to address, a war in progress cost the country thousands of lives on that fateful day. The possibilities of it happening again are far more likely than not. In my book, *Living Under The Patriot Act: Educating A Society,* I more than adequately outline the lineage of attacks by terrorists prior to 9-11. My articles on the subject of the Patriot Act, the most powerful tool today in the war against terrorism, deal primarily with the secondary enemies to American security. That enemy is readily apparent in the growing far left liberal base of the Democrat party.

As I have said before, the Democrat party has become the party of defeat beyond that of economics but to include our national security and the War on Terror. Defeating Bush has taken precedence against defeating economic challenges, such as inflation, to include the more important issue of terrorism. This is not such a heavy burden for Democrats to carry as one might think. As it stands, President Bush, no matter his shortcomings in economic spending, represents American fundamentals in direct opposition to the liberal philosophy when it comes to fighting a war.

Despite not implementing a strong border security policy, President Bush is a War Hawk who has no fear to go to war if he believes it is the only option to protect the country. The President stood tall and rejected the impotent and ineffective maneuvers of the United Nations that the Democrats so embrace. Do you know what I am talking about? It's the old threat and do nothing, threat and do nothing and repeat strategy that has made the United Nations the laughingstock of the world. In defiance of this interesting liberal strategy of self defense, the President took bold steps and created a coalition of the willing and did something the country does not always do, showed some backbone. My first article on the Patriot Act is short and sweet and to the point and was titled, *Why Democrats Fear The Patriot Act*. The article covers what I believe is an apparent lack of will to fight the War on Terror. You be the judge.

Why Democrats Fear The Patriot Act

Some may wonder why Democrats in the Senate filibustered the Patriot Act renewal. The mantra being forwarded by Senators like Russ Feingold is that the Patriot Act lacks the proper civil liberties safeguards and that his newly created "Coalition of Opposition" in the Senate serves to protect Americans from the tyrannical desires of the Bush administration. Several facts challenge the civil liberties thesis forwarded by Senators such as Feingold. The most obvious is the fact that the Patriot Act, in one way or another, has already been endorsed by most Democrats. Here are but a few examples: Janet Reno, Bill Clinton's Attorney General has publicly endorsed the USAPA. Bill Clinton himself used the now highly contentious section 215 of the USAPA as a centerpiece in his response to the 1995 Oklahoma City bombing. John Kerry is one of the contributing authors of the USAPA. The 9-11 commission stated that the Patriot Act was a valuable tool in the War on Terror. Of course it should be mentioned that there was an actual 98-1 vote in 2001 in the Senate on the USAPA in favor of the legislation. When you take these facts and add them to the plethora of other instances when Democrats have supported USAPA when it is convenient, the civil liberties reasoning for opposition starts getting very weak.

I believe that the true reason why Democrats fear, notice I did not say hate or dislike, the true reason they fear the USAPA is twofold. I subscribe to the long standing theory forwarded by many conservatives that through lack of inspiration and creativity, Democrats have failed to devise alternative strategies to the Bush administration's War on Terror. This mental idleness on the part of Democrats has forced them to oppose all aspects of the Bush agenda just to have some course of action to take. This thesis has been found to be viable as the actions of Democrats have been so repetitious and, in some cases, almost mindless in opposition to anything the President forwards.

However, when analyzing the actions of Democrats in the Senate on the issue of the Patriot Act, this theory alone is not satisfactory. I suggest that the reason the Democrats were willing to kill the Patriot Act, and the country's most substantial tool in the War on Terror to date, goes to the heart of the Democratic psyche. Yes, that inner core of self that is one component that makes the red states red and the blue states blue. The Patriot Act, with its safeguards in the forms of congressional oversight and sunsetting provisions, represents a symbol that strikes fear into the majority of Democrats. That symbol is action.

The Patriot Act, in its aggressive stance against terrorism, forces Democrats out of the realm of theory and into the more challenging realm of reality. This reality was brought to bear by President Bush in the form of the Patriot Act. The creation of the Patriot Act alone is a testament to the reality that the previous tactics in fighting terrorism were not working. The Patriot Act, as a symbol, can be seen as one of America's tools to "stand" against terrorism. Of course as with any true action, it could fail, it also has ramifications in the fact that it will actually do something. It is these side effects of the Patriot Act that do not set well with Democrats.

Supporting the Patriot Act does not come with an escape hatch or exit strategy for accountability. In addition, the Patriot Act is not a vague threat to terrorists shrouded in nuances, it's not another resolution, it's the big dog in the yard that bites. The fact that the Patriot Act has borne fruit and continues to have the majority support of the U.S. citizens is simply additional salt in the wound of an already dejected Democratic Party. Unfortunately, a one month reprieve for the Patriot Act will do nothing to change the psychological makeup for Democrats and, I fear, for the future of the law. It will take a groundswell of support for the USAPA from citizens across this country to re-channel the Democrats fear of action back to where it should be, on keeping their jobs. (Ibbetson, 2006, January 7)

My next article on the Patriot Act was originally published by my good friends at *Military Magazine*, www.milmag.com. I have never been able to find anyone who can't share a story from their youth about being afraid of a monster in their room when the lights went out. No matter where that creature hid, it was real to us, and really scared us to death. The article, *The Patriot Act: Searching for Monsters in the Closet,* is an attempt to address our mental perspectives on perceived threats from childhood to adulthood and how they relate to physical action. To avoid childhood flashbacks, keep the light on when you read this article, or maybe have your mom and dad over for the evening. My hope for conservatives is that we are ready to stand up together to eliminate our monsters. I hope I am right.

The Patriot Act: Searching for Monsters in the Closet

When you were young did you have a monster in your closet? Many a child has lost sleep to the monster that must certainly reside just inside the bedroom closet. If you reflect back on your monster, he probably was the end product of late night horror movies or creative tales spun with school buddies on late night sleepovers which are all fun and games with the boys until the monster actually comes to visit the next night when all your friends are conveniently gone. Now the thing about the closet monster is that he's crafty and clever. He won't show himself when friends are around and never in the daytime. No, he waits until your head is turned almost always to something else or, worse, when you're sound asleep. The closet monster has power, a power that can make you freeze for endless moments fearing that any slight motion might be the deciding factor in whether he will burst from the closet, which can only end in your certain death, or give you one more night's reprieve. Thank goodness a magical thing happens somewhere along life's path, we grow up. It does not happen all at once but, step by step, we gain perspective about what's real and what's not and the monster loses some of his power. Then on some special night this gained knowledge bolsters bravery to the point of a confrontation with the closet door and the monster is exposed for what he really is, nothing.

It would be nice to say that there are no monsters in real life, but that would not be true. As a nation, America has seen many monsters in many forms. Hitler's Nazi Germany and Tojo's Japan are but a few examples. America, although always diverse in thought and ideas, came together in a united effort to defeat these monsters in a time when indecision could have cost the country. We are at that crossroads again. While it is reasonable and logical to draw distinctions from World War II and The War on Terror, look at some of the similarities.

Hitler wanted to eliminate all groups of people not fitting the mold of the master Arian race. Al-Qaeda and other radical Islamic groups believe it is their mission to exterminate Israel and its ally, America, which both fall into the category of the Zionist unbelievers. Similarities are evident when looking at the Japanese kamikazes of World War II and the terrorist mentality of today that would propel a person to fly passenger planes into buildings, let alone strap explosives to one's own body. Yes, monsters have been around in the past and walk amongst us today.

Hitler's war walked across Europe taking country after country, forging deadly alliances and double crossing all those naïve to his deadly intentions. Al-Queda, under the leadership of Osama bin Laden, repeatedly attacked American interests (e.g. 1993 World Trade Bombing, 1995 U.S.S. Cole Bombing, Tanzania Embassy Bombing). Osama bin Laden funneled money to terrorist cells around the world for the purpose of Jihad. In 1941, America was struck with a devastating surprise attack at Pearl Harbor. On September 11, 2001, America was struck with a devastating surprise attack which surpassed the number of deaths suffered at Pearl Harbor. In both cases the country faced a monster that wanted to destroy us.

Unfortunately, America is not dealing with today's monsters the same way we have in the past. In fact, certain factions within the country would have you believe that the real monsters of today reside in the most illogical of places. Many civil rights groups portray the Patriot Act as this uncontrollable monster that roams the streets eating people's rights. This, despite the fact that after years of usage, there have been no documented cases of abuse with the law. In case that slipped by, I'll repeat it, NO ABUSES. The Patriot Act has been audited for abuses by many organizations including the ACLU. In fact, the Patriot Act has served to move national security forward by leaps and bounds by clarifying ambiguous laws, updating outdated laws, and yes, strengthening some older laws to help in fighting a new type of war.

Others have identified the President as the monster for everything from the usage of NSL's to when the winds blow the wrong way. Any attempt to challenge these naysayers with facts is met with the usual accusations that "fruitful debate" is being quashed. Meanwhile time passes with division, indecision, and worst of all, inaction. The failure of the Patriot Act to be renewed after the creation of a compromise package bill was a glaring example of the difference in how many Democrats feel the War on Terror should be prosecuted.

Surpassing the issue of the Patriot Act renewal, Democrats have set a dangerous precedent in time of war by the actions of the "Coalition of Opposition." Our enemies are coordinated and motivated. Their agenda is clear, destroy America. The impression given by Congress' inability to come together on legislation for fighting terrorism, and the willingness of some to kill the Patriot Act altogether to make political points with fringe liberal groups, will be seen by our enemies as a sign of weakness. We know that Hitler advanced on those who appeared weak; we should expect no less from fanatical terrorist groups. Democrats have failed to learn what all children come to terms with, that is, eventually you have to deal with monsters. (Ibbetson, 2006, January 28)

If we are to defeat our enemies in the War on Terror we must come to terms with the fact that we are fighting a new kind of warfare. No longer do our enemies have set borders and an easy to find zip code. The enemies of today work in stealth-like terrorist cells and reducing their threat will take years. If we as a nation are to stand strong over time to this threat, we must be able to rally around our national security efforts. This does not mean turning a blind eye to government and government's effects on civil liberties. It does require Americans to realize the long-term struggle and the need for sacrifice. I believe that it also requires our recognition of groups whose sole function is to tear the country to pieces for a personal agenda.

Groups like the ACLU, a communist founded organization, should be identified and held to account. During war, their detrimental effects to the nation are multiplied. My last article on the Patriot Act uses one of my favorite childhood movies, *The Goonies*, to properly show the ACLU's true reasons for their Patriot Act opposition in the usage of national security letters. I believe, if your eyes are open, you will find a monster in this article, and a deadly one indeed.

Feeding the Beast

It's time to feed the beast! The feeding of the beast scenario comes in many forms and we have all heard it in one variation or another. In general terms, the beast is that dark sinister creature that lurks in the dank nether regions, restrained only by the most meager of barriers, is always ready to strike, and yes, always hungry. One of my personal favorite renditions of the feeding of the beast story is in the 1985 Warner Brother's movie *The Goonies*.

Within the storyline of the movie, the loveable character "Chunk" attempts to "feed the beast" that has been kept chained in the dark, dank, basement of the bandit's hideout. Unfortunately, unlike *The Goonies* version, the beast seldom is portrayed as the misunderstood sweet anomaly with a heart of gold. No, the beast most often is a hungry killer, a creature that if not kept shackled and constrained will consume all within its reach. The feeding of the beast scenario is currently being spun within the media accounts of the FBI National Security Letter debacle. Those without fear please continue.

As many know, FBI Director Robert Mueller has come forth to admit that the usage of National Security Letters, whose authority has been expanded by the controversial Patriot Act, has been mishandled. These reports have brought to light the failure of the FBI to record approximately 8,500 official requests for information (Jordan, 2007). These transgressions were documented within a 126 page audit conducted by Inspector General Glen A. Fine. Fine would report that agents had collected information through the usage of National Security Letters, at times without official authority (Jordan, 2007). There is little question about the accuracy of the Fine report; in fact, FBI Director Mueller's acknowledgement of his own accountability in the procedural breakdown only further validates the findings. The question is, what are we really looking at? Is this a case of poor training and execution of policy or has the beast finally been exposed? The ACLU would tell you that it is the latter. The radical activist organization said that the justice department audit is proof positive that the Patriot Act must again go under the knife to be amended (Jordan, 2007). Anthony D. Romero, the ACLU's Executive Director, said, 'The attorney general and the FBI are part of the problem, and they cannot be trusted to be part of the solution' (Jordan, 2007. ¶ 18). This is an all too familiar tune from the organization that has opposed the Patriot Act at every level since its creation. One can almost hear the ACLU preparations for battle with the beast in: the oiling of the torches, the sharpening of the pitchforks, the typing of Republican resignation request letters, and of course, the coordination e-mails with the Democrat party. A hunting we will go, a hunting we will go....

Oddly enough, not everyone sees "the beast" in this National Security Letter story. Michael C. Dorf, professor of law at Columbia University, while showing his concern for the need to have accountability within government activities, sees the FBI breakdown as an example of sloppiness from overwork and improper training (Dorf, 2007). The worst misuse, as reported by Dorf, came in the form of violations of FBI internal guidelines stated within contracts with three internet providers (Dorf, 2007). Dorf states, and I would agree, that there appears to be no evidence of deliberate abuse for political purpose or criminal conduct in this case. These findings would be consistent with Inspector General Glenn A. Fine's investigation (Jordan, 2007). However, I believe that the FBI's sloppiness and general bungling of department procedure is a shortcoming that cannot be accepted. Dorf's comparison of holding the government accountable to at least the standards of the business model of performance is completely valid. While FBI Director Robert S. Mueller has stated that he has not been requested to resign (Jordan, 2007), I would not be surprised if we do not see his exit sometime in the near future. It would seem logical that his ability to effectively administrate should be the yardstick by which his employment is evaluated. Regardless of the fate of Mueller, the ability of the FBI to expedite corrections to its procedures for issuing NSL's is paramount and will go far in restoring the FBI's credibility. There is certainly some hard work to be done but it is a far cry from "the beast" scenario in which the ACLU continually portrays the Patriot Act.

Ironically, I agree with the ACLU that an actual "beast" does exist in this country. You can forget the monster in the closet which is kids stuff compared to the beast that has been roaming the foundations of this country. This beast is always hungry and the dining courses it demands come in the form of: our border security, Christian values, our American pride, and our national identity. Unfortunately, the beast has been fed very well for many years. I think that the ACLU would be most suited to track this vile beast down. I would simply tell them to collect their gear and begin their quest in front of a mirror, and with parting words of encouragement, I would say, "Happy Hunting!" (Ibbetson, 2007, March 21)

References

Dorf, M. A. (2007, March 14). The FBI's misuse of national security letters reveals the often-false dichotomy between security and privacy. *FindLaw*. Retrieved March 16, 2007, from http://writ.news. findlaw.com/dorf/20070314.html

Ibbetson, P. A. (2006, January 7). Why democrats fear the Patriot Act. *American Daily*. Retrieved from http://www.americandaily. com/article/11100

Ibbetson, P. A. (2006, January 28). The Patriot Act: Searching for monsters in the closet. *American Daily*. Retrieved from http://www. americandaily.com/article/11532

Ibbetson, P. A. (2007, March 21). Feeding the beast. *The Land of the Free*. Retrieved from http://www.thelandofthefree.net/conservativeopinion/2007/03/23/feeding-the-beast/

Jordan, L. J. (2007, March 9). Gonzales, Mueller admit FBI broke law. *Breitbart*. Retrieved March 11, 2007, from http://www.breitbart. com/article.php?id=D8NP15BO0&show_article=1

Chapter 7

Why Zoos Have Fences

DID YOU EVER WONDER WHY the zoo is fenced in? Our first knee-jerk reaction might be a concern for what the animals might do to us. Movies like the Robin William's classic, Jumanji, give us all a vivid picture of wild animals running around town causing catastrophe after catastrophe among the city folk. While movies like that are entertaining, do you think that they really reflect reality? That is, if all the fences fell down in the middle of the night, would the animals at your local zoo take control of your town by sun up? I really doubt it. Actually, due to the fact that liberals have failed to take away the people's right to bear arms, if all the animals were to break free tonight, the trophy rooms around this country would probably be greatly enlarged. When it comes down to it, fencing at the zoo protects the zoo community from those outside its perimeter.

Countries do the same thing; they fence in and protect their citizens, their culture, and their way of life from outside invaders. Yes, countries all around the world do that, but not America. Caught in one of the most vicious applications of political correctness, liberals have been winning their war on our border security. Hey, let's be fair, you say. Okay, from the perspective of political parties, both Republicans and Democrats are to blame. Republicans have winked at the problem of border security to continue to receive cheap labor while Democrats are looking for new voters for the future. You say illegal aliens can't vote. My answer is, not yet.

Validating the differences between conservatism and liberalism within the political parties, conservatives like Duncan Hunter and Tom Tancredo have fought both Republicans and Democrats tooth and nail to secure our borders. I believe that border security is the biggest national security issue

93

of our time. Once again, the fundamental principles of conservatism separate those for and against border security no matter what political party they lay claim to. I forward the simple logic that it is in everyone's best interest to create a secure border now as opposed to after another terrorist attack. Liberals put your thinking caps on for a moment. Fear government oppression and overreaction in border security? Do you think that you're avoiding such oppression at the border by opposing any measures to secure the country? What do you think will happen WHEN we are attacked again and the attack is tracked back to an open border? Can your logic see the potential for an overreaction by the government to secure the border in the direct aftermath of a terrorist attack as opposed to it being implemented now? I say it with all kindness, liberals, you're guaranteeing what you fear while also placing Americans that don't agree with you at risk. Well, I've put liberals once again in their place, now it's time to see where the buck stops.

While I am a public supporter of President Bush and proudly display the letter he sent me on March 30, 2007, on my Patriot Act book, *Living Under The Patriot Act: Educating A Society,* on my living room wall, it is only fair to critique his performance as President in all the arenas for which he is responsible. While I praise the President on many issues, border security is not one of them. I feel that U.S. border security, at this point in time, is nothing short of a joke. Not only has the administration failed to show the political grit necessary to fight Democrat and Republican opposition, they have also undermined the assistance of patriots, such as the Minutemen, who have sacrificed their time, money, and reputations to secure the southern border. I have met Jim Gilchrist, president and founder of the Minutemen, and I spoke with him at length about the issue of border security. I found Mr. Gilchrist to be an honest man whose movement to secure our open borders has assisted in keeping this paramount issue in the forefront of the public eye. I've met with smaller but just as significant border security organizations, such as the Texas Border Regulators under the direction of President Paul McWilliams. The Texas Border Regulators assist border patrol agents through spotting and calling authorities as illegal aliens enter the country in the area of El Paso, Texas. The Texas Border Regulators accept no donations and work completely out of their own pocket. I found their work spirit and love for country to be inspirational.

While the noble sacrifices of citizens such as Gilchrist and McWilliams and all those who work with them show that America has not totally lost a concern over border security, their efforts would not be necessary if the government would simply fulfill one of their most basic functions, securing the borders. It seems so simple an issue that a child could figure it out. In that vein I take readers inside the kitchen to observe some simple rules you will all remember while taking the President to task on this important issue.

Border Security Strategies from the Kitchen

"Clean your plate!" Remember this parental mantra? It is likely that you, like most children, underwent this unique educational experience. For parents, using the kitchen as a classroom; that is, teaching children to "clean their plate" (eat all their food) was a lesson that goes far beyond simple grocery economics. In reality, parents teach their children the valuable ethics of responsibility — children learn that both lunch and life are full of tasks that must be completed. Furthermore, the plate cleaning process teaches children to take personal responsibility for finishing a given task. Parents teach their children to focus their attention not on the "plate cleaning" status of other siblings, but on taking ownership of the lunchtime process as a personal matter. This new reality, and the impact of taking personal responsibility, are driven home when the child is faced with the dreaded obstacle of an unwanted piece of cauliflower or broccoli that must be eaten. It is in these trying times that the child learns some very important lessons that will benefit him or her in adulthood. In essence, children learn that when the going gets tough, you often have to suck it up, hold your nose, and face the undesirable task.

We see many similarities in the kitchen "plate cleaning" challenge that are also present in our nation's challenge to protect the border. Currently, the issue of border security has been pushed into the forefront of public debate. This is an issue that has been lingering on America's plate for a long time. However, since September 11, 2001, a sense of urgency to deal with the issue of border security has been rekindled. For decades, those who have petitioned for tighter border security have cited the economic strain that illegal aliens place on domestic jobs and social services. Others point to the impact of crime that occurs when criminals from others countries are allowed to run unchecked and un-monitored amongst the U.S. populace. The current dilemma of an unprotected border now includes the terrorist agent(s) and the fear building tools of terrorism, such as (WMD) Weapons of Mass Destruction. Despite having a strong defensive strategy abroad for fighting terrorism, America's unwillingness to secure the border leaves the country with a full plate of problems. Based from a historical lack of political will, America can be likened to a stubborn child, who by failing to cleanse his plate, must sit with his food and wait for things to get so unbearable that action is finally taken. The very same thing that makes the stubborn child's standoff so aggravating to the parent is the same factor that makes border security advocates angry with the government. That is, in both cases, the end goal could be achieved within a few simple steps. That is, true border security implementation, like plate cleaning, is not brain surgery; the challenge is in having the will to complete the task. As with both tasks, it is suggested that the simple but valuable logic of "A few bites and you're done" be forwarded. That is, break the task into simple steps that, linked together, achieve the desired goal.

The recipe for true border security is obvious and simple: construct permanent physical barriers across the entire border, deploy the military to the border with full detention authority, and create a strict but fair immigration program for the future. Failing to implement all of these programs will deny the country a truly secure border leaving the problem for others to deal with. It is easy to fall into the liberal trap that all issues are complex. If one falls into this mental "Bermuda triangle," simple constructions (such as a wall) must be analyzed as to the possible "statement" someone on the opposite side of the hemisphere may associate with it. Of course a wall does make a statement, "Don't go past this point!" However, the failings of liberal-minded deliberation on border security is that it is perceived that action cannot be taken unless it benefits border countries as much, if not more, than the

U.S. This can, and usually does, lead to inaction or just plan silly action.

The challenge of creating border security has now been laid upon the President's plate. Will the President deal with the problem once and for all? Will the problem simply be swept to the side of the plate and be followed by a Presidential statement of "all done"? There is no doubt that some will dispute securing the border. The current protests in many large cities mark a bizarre version of that opposition in which illegal aliens demand the rights of U.S. citizens. There is bound to be additional opposition to securing the border from the Mexican government. From our kitchen analogy, this is the perfect time to avoid worrying if Mexico will clean its own plate. We know the answer to this question. Regardless of the opposition, the need for action is real, the objective is obvious, and the time is now. Mr. President, secure the border and end the decades of useless, cyclical talk about border security. Don't pass the problem on to another administration to deal with — clean your plate! (Ibbetson, 2006, May 19)

Every conservative who has championed the secure border cause has, at some point, been called or categorized as a foe of the poor immigrant. This argument, of course, is based on the silent but dangerously naïve assumption that somehow there is an invisible barrier at the border that allows the poor immigrant to pass unforeseen into the country while blocking the sex offender, drug dealer, gang member, and terrorist entrance. The article *Border Security: The Ugly Side of Compassion* was written to break through liberal hypocrisy on this issue and show just who is the dealer of compassion and who the dealer of deception.

Border Security: The Ugly Side of Compassion

It's time to start showing compassion when implementing border security strategies. What did that statement mean to you? In reality, when talking about securing the border, the term compassion means different things to different people. In fact, to make the previous utterance for compassion in the public forum would most certainly create a chain reaction of both "gasps" and "sighs." For conservatives, the knee-jerk reaction is to see the idea of compassion as a liberal inroad to avoiding border control implementation altogether. In reality, the nature of liberal compassion is a much uglier thing. Liberals have a tendency to publicly designate conservative propositions for border security as simply draconian measures that punish the poor and downtrodden foreigner who is simply looking for a better life. It is within the area of compassion that liberals claim the moral high ground and often claim an unchallenged victory by default over conservatives. I say that conservatives should step forward aggressively on this issue and challenge liberals on what they believe is their holy high ground. I will do so now.

At the foundational level, liberals and conservatives see compassion from radically different perspectives. Conservatives see compassion from the perspective of allowing people an even playing field upon which those that wish to aspire to a higher level can do so with hard work. Liberals simply shake their heads at these notions as they see individuals as perpetually helpless victims who, by a terminal lack of economic mobility, must rely on big government for their every need. This philosophy of helplessness shapes itself into the border issue and quickly the ugly side of compassion starts to rear its head. First, for liberals, securing the border with compassion ultimately means to leave the border completely open. To limit anyone, including al-Qaeda from strolling into the U.S. at will is repugnant to the liberal psyche. This comes in part due to the backward nature of liberalism itself. Within this mentality, for compassion to be effective, it requires programs that force America to frequently take it on the chin. This unpublicized belief system stems from the fact that liberals see America as the overbearing bully of the world who needs to be taken down a notch from time to time. Much of this lingering American hatred stems from a resentment that capitalism was never plucked away by the masses as prognosticated by liberal heroes such as Karl Marx. This silent self-loathing of America breaks the surface from time to time for all to see.

There is little wonder why the argument made by border security advocates of the financial drain on social services caused by illegal aliens flooding across a porous border has had no impact in the liberal sphere. By the simple socialistic nature of liberalism, the thought of reducing the flow of governmental entitlement to anyone is seen as the ultimate taboo. It would be overboard to say that liberals want the ultimate destruction of America; however, a financial drain here, a terrorist attack there, are often internalized by the liberal mind as something America should expect and take graciously and we surely have it coming. It is by understanding the liberal mind that one can begin to comprehend how the liberals' delegate "compassion" to some and not to others. Compassion is seen as a commodity; that is, something to be sold to the highest bidder. The highest bidders under this warped scheme are those that are the most helpless. Notice I did not say the most in need nor the most worthy. That is why, once again to the liberal, living in an America that flies a flag void of the hammer and sickle is such a challenge. Thus, with the daily burden of living in an America not of their choosing, delegating compassion at the expense of the country as a whole is seen as therapeutic. Specific to the border issue, making the U.S. citizen, as well as the documented alien suffer both economically by the strain to social services, or physically by the threat of terrorism, are seen as acts of compassion because it's just putting America in its place. This is the ugly side of liberal compassion that I say should be illuminated.

When confronted with the overwhelming challenge of legitimizing open borders with national security, national sovereignty, or domestic social services, liberals quickly retreat to their high ground; that is, their holy hill of compassion. I say that it is time they die on that hill. With careful aim, a final arrow is shot at the argument that having an open border is a true form of compassion to the illegal alien. Under the current system, the illegal alien is by default labeled as part criminal, part indentured servant, and now potential terrorist as well. It is the covert nature of the illegal alien, created by an absolute lack of identification, that has been the driving force behind many of these categorizations. However, this is only the tip of the deadly iceberg. To see the total lack of compassion that open borders have on illegal aliens, one has only to quickly compare the U.S. citizen with the illegal alien. In contrast to the U.S. citizen, the illegal alien works for the lowest wage with no benefits. This individual moves about the country open to all legal sanctions of U.S. law with no voice or representation regarding those laws. One could say that the illegal alien in the U.S. walks in the constant shadow of the Damocles sword. Is this the compassion that liberals tout? Having a porous border also releases the Mexican government from any responsibility to create any viable economic infrastructure domestically. Recognizing these facts is not a call for amnesty but a call for true compassion. That is, compassion that starts with America itself and then extends to its visitors. When America respects its own borders, laws, and sovereignty, its visitors will do the same. With that said, the battleground for true compassion in border security is still internal. It is a battle of conservative and liberal ideologies. Border security strategies will continue to follow the victor of this ideological struggle. For conservatives, our strategy for victory on the issue of border security should go beyond our belief that people will become frustrated with liberals using hope as a defense and apathy as a strategy for securing the border. Our strategy must also include articulating the conservative ideals within border security that by its nature creates an environment in which true compassion can flourish.

For conservatives, the final message is that the debate over border security needs to expand to encompass the more broad nature of the liberal fallacy of compassion. This has been the downfall of many conservative arguments on border security. One must not fail to articulate that truly secure borders show the world that a country respects itself and has compassion for its own people. This is the true foundation for forwarding compassion to others who come to work and live in America. Conservatives cannot be content to hold familiar grounds (national security) in this battle of ideologies. If we really want to win the debate for a secure border, we must advance forward on the issue of compassion; we must send arrows into all the enemy's strongholds. It is here that the liberal ideology of compassion can be exposed as the ugly thing it is. (Ibbetson, 2006, May 30)

References

Ibbetson, P. A. (2006, May 19). Border security strategies from the kitchen. *News By Us*. Retrieved from http://newsbyus.com/more. php?id=A3588_0_1_0_M

Ibbetson, P. A. (2006, May 30). Border security: The ugly side of compassion. *News By Us*. Retrieved from http://newsbyus.com/more. php?id=A3752_0_1_0_M

Chapter 8

Noticing The Zebra's Stripes

HAVE YOU EVER WONDERED WHAT would happen if those beautiful black and white stripped zebras were to lose their stripes? Did you know that the stripes on zebras are an intricate part of their survival as it confuses predators during their attacks? So, in effect, taking away the zebra's stripes would most likely cause their eventual death. In the end, zebras just have to be zebras. For conservatives it's the same thing. We are who we are and I would have it no other way. While the fundamentals of conservatism could thrive in any political party, it has been for many decades found under the umbrella of the Republican Party.

However, with that being said, the Republican Party, at times, has failed to maintain its fundamental conservative foundations. This has happened for many reasons. Over the last several years Republicans have, to a degree, lost themselves while trying to reach across the cage in the name of compromise to a liberal Democratic Party for compromises they believe will be reciprocated down the road. This shows a naiveté that, from the sidelines, most conservative spectators can discern at a glance. Liberals don't compromise, they dominate and win. To think compromise with Democrats can be attained on the most important issues this country faces shows a lack of political wisdom that questions why we have Republicans like this in office. You've learned, from the view of the fundamental principles of conservatism: (1) God, (2) Family, and (3) Country, that often these principles run completely counter to the views of liberals. When these major issues are addressed, compromise means that somebody won, and somebody was duped out of understanding that they lost.

The issues addressed in this book are major issues that will affect the direction of this country in the future, and they are issues that conservatives must control if this nation is to remain strong. I think voters recognize weakness and show their anger at the ballot box. In fact, in late 2006, voters went to the polls and punished Republicans then in office for straying from the conservative fundamentals they were placed there to preserve. Don't get me wrong, some very good Republicans were lost in the landslide voting punishments the public dealt out; however, I feel little sadness at the overall outcome as I, too, feel that Republicans of late have become far too spineless in defending superior conservative values. The article, *The Wrong Side of Ten,* is a hard hitting analysis of what happens when you get fat and lazy in the political fight to preserve this wonderful country.

The Wrong Side of Ten

Eight! Nine! Ten! These numbers may not have any immediate importance to the average person but, to the boxer, these numbers are magical. For as we all know, to a superficial extent, the boxer trains and hones his skill for an eventual confrontation that allows for only one victor. Within this context, the numbers, Eight! Nine! and Ten! mark the pivotal moments before the boxer feels the joy of victory or the agony of defeat. We have recently watched a battle of a different kind in which the main event, featured November 7, 2006, was in the form of the mid-term political elections. Different from the physical contest of the pugilists, this conflict centers over a choice of ideologies in which the hearts and minds of the nation are placed in the hands of a precious few individuals who are intended to vote the conscience of the country.

In case you were out of town, the fighter in the left corner wearing the blue trunks and weighing in at the massive weight of big 'government' won the fight, and won it big time. That's right, and no amount of re-winds or fast-forwards from your video machine can take away the knock-out punch that the Democrats laid on the Republican Party that fateful night. It was important to wait for the emotions of the November 7, 2006, election results to wane before analyzing the ramifications of this defeat. The hope is to avoid the angry disjointed ramblings that we often hear during boxing matches from both the winners and losers minutes after the fight has been completed, when the smoke is still thick and the flash bulbs are popping like machine gun fire. I believe that now is the time to calmly deal with what may have been the causes of the defeat, and more importantly, what I would forward as the recipe for a comeback in 2008.

There is little doubt, for those that live in reality, that the Republican Party has been the undisputed champion for more than the last six years. In fact, the Republicans held the majority of governorships, senator positions, controlled the House of Representatives, the Senate, and the high office of President of the United States all at once until the last election. I would argue that Republicans have held the belt because of their general adherence to the superior fundamentals of conservatism. However, if this is true, one must address why Republicans were found flat on their backs staring at the stars on Election Day? To answer these questions Republicans have to take a hard look at themselves and their goals for the future. Inevitably, the party is at the same crossroad as many a prize fighting champion who finds himself on the "Wrong Side of Ten." Republicans, like the boxer must assess the following questions before moving on to the next contest:

1. Was this loss simply a fluke, like we see in the ring with the phantom punch that denotes luck more than strategy?
2. Is it time to train differently and change tactics in an attempt to challenge the opponent's strengths, i.e. when the clubber attempts to become an agile boxer?
3. Was this loss due to being simply out of shape and underestimating the competition?
4. Is it time to hang it up?

Of course I would reject the idea that the principles of conservatism, which include the love of country, defense of the nation, and traditional Christian values, among others, should ever be abandoned. In fact, in many ways the display of conservative values by Democrats in the recent election, such as the campaign promotion of: pro-gun rights, anti-abortion rights, as well as the espousal of Christian values, were fundamental in several election wins. Talk about the rope-a-dope, which brings us back to the painful fact that Republicans sorely underestimated, their competition. This underestimation, however, can only be seen as a by-product of a fighter who gets a little lazy. Winning is a powerful thing, a wonderful thing, but also a deceptive thing. It is deceptive in the fact that a champion may start to feel invincible and that's usually the beginning of the end. For Republicans, it's time to go back to the gym, cut some flab, and get back to basics.

Republicans have no need to redefine themselves, that would be foolish and the end of the party. What is needed is a total recommitment to what won the belt in the first place and that is total dedication to conservative values. No compromises and no searching for a middle ground with those who would wish to destroy us both economically, socially, morally, and militarily. Yes, the lean fighter is a focused fighter who is willing to learn new things, but never forgets where his greatest strengths lie. To stay fit there must be no political correctness in the training films, and no moral relativism for dessert. We must remember that to stay in fighting shape is not enough as conservatives are not looking for competitors but for champions. Now that's a tough regimen to follow in today's world and that's why not everyone can wear the belt. Of course this request for excellence goes far beyond the politician; in fact, it is really a call to the public because, in reality, we are the promoters and trainers of who will send forth our fighters into the ring in 2008. The responsibility for conservatives, the mainstream of society, is not only to test our potential champions, but also to cut those who do not make the grade. As well, we must never stop teaching the next generations why the battle of ideologies remains as important today as it has throughout history. Lastly, we must all show up on fight night, in superior numbers, to the opposition in 2008 as we cannot afford to again find ourselves on the "Wrong Side of Ten." (Ibbetson, 2007, January 2)

References

Ibbetson, P. A. (2007, January 2). The wrong side of ten. *American Daily.* Retrieved from http://www.americandaily.com/article/17032

Chapter 9

Sounding The Dinner Bell: Adventures In Radio

YOU KNOW, WHEN YOU WANT to feed the animals, it's often routine to shake the proverbial bucket, sound the bell, or just let out a big holler to get the animals moving. In short, there needs to be a way to get the word out to as many as possible in the most efficient manner. This book is but another way of doing that and it is hoped that my humble attempts at humor, combined with the absolute seriousness of the issues being discussed, will be a fruitful combination that will inspire future thought on important issues and keep you turning the pages. In the process of sharing my conservative philosophy with readers, I have shared parts of my personal life to portray my quest to stress the fundamental battle taking place between liberal and conservative ideologies in this country. I have come to believe that if conservatives are to save this nation from the daily onslaught of moral relativism and communistic dogma that is challenging Americans for supremacy of their hearts and minds, then all the weapons of truth must be brought forth and implemented.

There is no doubt in my mind that the pen is mightier than the sword, and I have had the chance to publish many articles on various news and political websites that have stimulated debate and deep thinking on a wide range of political issues. What I have recently discovered is an extremely powerful tool that, if used properly, has the potential to make all the difference in this most important battle. That tool is radio.

For many lifelong radio listeners you already know how important radio is, to not only educate individuals, but also to inspire us to take action on important issues. What I can share is the importance I have found, from behind the microphone in the radio station setting, and its impact on my life as a conservative.

This process of discovering the world of radio hosting came in stages. It began when I was a tentative radio guest for my first book, *Living Under The Patriot Act: Educating a Society*. I learned early in the book marketing process that people listen to radio and if a person can market their ideas there, people will respond. At first I had the same fears that seize so many people when it comes to speaking in public forums. I wondered if the public would care about a book written on the subject of the Patriot Act and, maybe more importantly, I wondered if people would embrace the message coming from me. My preparation was simple and again embodied the conservative philosophy. First, I practiced like crazy. Even with that practice, I felt my first few radio programs were a little mechanical. What I avoided early on was to become depressed or lay any blame for my initial mistakes on others. In other words, I was not going to embrace the victimization philosophy that is so pervasive in liberalism today. As far as I was concerned, radio was new ground and I was going to have to master it, one interview at a time. Within a short time I began to feel more comfortable behind the microphone and I could feel the excitement of the radio experience among the radio hosts and callers as I went from show to show. As I continued the process as a radio guest, the feedback was so positive that I took a hard look at attempting to make the transition from radio guest to radio host.

It doesn't matter if your goals are to be an astronaut, radio host, or President for that matter; no one starts at the top. You have to work your way up. That's an important fact of life that liberals often overlook and it's part of the reason why we have such discontent and blame being thrown at society for an individual's failure. Simply put, liberals today have bypassed hard work for entitlement. For my radio debut, I started with a simple forum in Blog Talk Radio. This online free forum allows anyone to use the internet to have discussion on topics of interest. I had no investment costs other than my time, and I was able to familiarize myself with some of the simple switchboard procedures that are more complex in bigger operations. As important, I learned some of the valuable marketing skills needed to promote a radio style show and that all levels are competitive. Blog Talk Radio also helped me meet many wonderful conservatives with whom I still collaborate today.

After spending some time honing my skills with Blog Talk Radio, I moved to the next level. The question was where do I go from Blog Talk Radio? Again, I was an unconnected farm boy from Kansas so nothing was going to be given to me. I had to go get it myself. As I looked at my limited options, a door just seemed to open in front of me. I was at Kansas State University working on my Ph.D and I noticed the University had a college radio station where students could apply for their own shows. There is no doubt that universities are one of the last strong liberal bastions and I wondered if a true conservative talk show would even be tolerated, much less flourish, but the opportunity was there and I wasn't going to let it go by without fighting for a chance to move to the next level of radio. I showed up for an interview and pitched my show along with eight other prospective shows, all competing for only two open slots. In the end, I won the Tuesday slot and the *Conscience of Kansas* radio show was born.

My format for the program was simple, learn the technology, get great guests, and tell the truth at all costs. There is little doubt that this was another big boost as I was beyond the internet listenership of Blog Talk Radio and was now being heard on car radios and in living rooms in most of Northeast Kansas. However, there were still those who said that large scale success in radio was unattainable. I heard individuals, even within the university radio department, who pushed the liberal philosophy of defeat, saying no one listens to college radio and no upscale guests would come on these shows. I shrugged off the naysayers as I was too busy trying to make the most of my opportunity.

After learning the intricacies of the technology within the college radio forum, it all came down to my ability to communicate with people in a way that brings them back week after week wanting to hear more. The foundation of a great show is to tell the truth, regardless of whether this creates tons of hate mail or lavishes a person with the praises of others. People are not stupid and they understand consistency and honesty and they can smell a fraud a mile away.

The flavor of a show, as I like to call it, comes from the guests and the callers. This is where I learned that the myth I was fed early in college radio, that good guests could not be acquired, was simply not true. With hard work and a certain amount of creativity, the *Conscience of Kansas* radio program began to bring in some of the biggest names in the country. Some guests who have appeared on the show include Jim Gilchrist of the *Minutemen Project;* Melanie Morgan of *Move America Forward;* Kristinn Taylor of the Washington DC branch of the *FreeRepublic*; Jerome Corsi, bestselling author of *Unfit for Command* and the *Obama Nation*; Lieutenant Colonel Buzz Patterson, bestselling author of *War Crimes*; Sheriff Joe Arpaio, known as the *Toughest Sheriff in America*; David Freddoso, author of *The Case Against Barack Obama*; bestselling author Ronald Kessler; and terrorism and Islamic specialists such as Dr. Walid Phares and Robert Spencer, are just a few of the big names I have had join me on the program.

Having some of the best known guests in the country was a huge step forward and I worked to get the program replayed on other radio stations throughout the week. Still, there was room for improvement and that's when videotaping was launched. Now some would say that you can't really do any video work without a big budget and tons of highly paid specialists with high tech equipment. Here, again, I had to shrug off this negative thinking and look positively ahead to the challenge of how to get my conservative message out to as many people as possible. I had a simple home video camera that I took to the radio station and placed on a stack of CDs until it was face level and I pushed the record button. That simple. But just as important, the videos appearing through the free service at YouTube. com has opened up the Conscience of Kansas radio program to thousands of people who did not know the program existed.

It was about the same time I began videotaping shows that I learned the value of debating villains on the radio. Previously I had been debating angry liberal callers but I had never really tangled with hostile guests on my show. On April 29, 2008, a landmark was made when I interviewed Shirley Phelps Roper of the Kansas cult known as the Westboro Baptist Church. Feel free to view the interview, in two parts, at: http://www.youtube.com/watch?v=yF3DkYIjo6A and http://www.youtube.com/watch?v=ZMQ1riSJp6Y. It was not a perfect taping as the guest called in late and we ran out of tape before the show was over, but from the overwhelming video viewership of the two segments we had, which still continues to receive new viewers every week, another important lesson was learned – if a person is fortunate enough to have a forum like radio, it must be used from time to time to directly challenge those who would damage this country. On a fundamental level, I think people want to see conservatives stand up and fight for what they believe. After the Westboro showdown I was overwhelmed with positive listener mail and it has had an impact on the show's format.

Don't get me wrong, I don't believe that radio should be a playground for political "hit men." I am simply saying that I won't shy away from a legitimate fight for fear of bringing a little anger on the radio waves. What I have done is professionalized the process by incorporating debate interviews with video and these videos are now embedded within my writing as an independent columnist.

This newest facet of combining radio with the writing of articles turned out to be very helpful in disseminating the truth. On June 24, 2008, I published in *World Net Daily*, one of the largest conservative publications in the nation, my observations of an interview with Code Pink Co-founder Jodie Evans. This was solid proof that foes such as Code Pink could be faced and beaten in a public forum, but more importantly that this information could spread across the nation if the proper mechanism were in place. In the political avalanche that followed my June 24th interview, the interview was cited as part of an official press release by the Republican National Committee, *Washington Post, Front Page Magazine, Hot Air*, and the list goes on and on. Not only did I learn that a little conservative radio show from Kansas could make national waves and expose the communist nature of Code Pink, I learned as well that if you had a quality product, big name guests would come to you. This is one of the first rewards I saw for success in radio. It is here that I want to share my article on Code Pink that was published on *World Net Daily* in which we first used embedded video links.

From Pink to Red

As momentum continues to build in the aftermath of my radio interview with Jodie Evans of Code Pink, I thought I would take a few moments to reflect publicly on my own personal observations of what took place in this unique conversation. I call it a unique conversation because I believe, for a brief moment, the public was privy to an uncensored view of the communistic philosophy from the leadership of Code Pink.

It would only be fair to tell you how this interview transpired. I originally contacted Medea Benjamin regarding an interview on my radio show, "Conscience of Kansas." Benjamin said she would be out of the country, but gave me the contact information of Jodie Evans. After lengthy deliberations with her assistant, we hedged out the content questions for the interview and the date and time of the show was set. Pretty simple stuff, right? For most purposes the interview was in a simple conversational style. I invite everyone to listen to the interview in full from our archives at www.ibbetsonusa.com where it can be listened to commercial free or downloaded. Video portions are available at YouTube.com http://www.youtube.com/watch?v=O758gyZqxlw and http://www.youtube.com/watch?v=J5dSWfl331U and I welcome everyone to take a long hard look at what was said; however, I doubt that Evans would extend the same invitation.

I've interviewed hundreds of people in my life, either as a police investigator or behind the microphone, and a lot about an individual can be discovered by how they act during simple conversations. When interviewing criminals, it is often the contradictions in the statements they make that eventually lead to their undoing and the truth of the criminal matter being exposed. This is applicable to the Evans interview in that she was a treasure trove of contradictions.

Evans said she supports the military but wants them to limit their recruitment capabilities. She said she is the most patriotic military supporter she knows (she should get out more). Evans says that Code Pink does not support communism, but their organization is full of communist supporters, and the leader she holds in highest esteem is the communist dictator Hugo Chavez. These contradictions, in my opinion, reflect the personal conflict that Evans struggled with when we spoke. The conflicts were evident in what she "wanted" to say and what she felt she "should" say in a public forum. Fortunately, for truth's sake, her lack of self control, which led to her use of profanity on the air and her chronic interruptions of my questions, also led to moments where she spoke from her heart. This was where the pink turned to red and where we glimpsed the truly ugly communistic American hating side of Code Pink's leadership.

In the middle of a spirited exchange, Evans validated the 9-11 attacks committed by Osama bin Laden. When I challenged her on this point I could feel Evan's personal conflict with the truth. She eventually opted to back pedal from the clear concise statement she had just made. This conflict with the truth was present again when I questioned Evans about Code Pink's affiliation with Communism. She was extremely reluctant to answer these questions and made a valiant attempt to convince me that being a communist and being a good American could be tied together. Sorry Jodie, I did not buy that argument then and I do not buy it now.

Criticisms of how I handled Jodie Evans continue as this interview has rapidly become a part of the public consciousness. Some critics feel I was too easy on Evans and allowed her to bully her way during the interview. Others believe that had I engaged in the verbal brawl she apparently wanted, I would have simply sunk to her level and demeaned myself. I think there is some truth to both statements; however, I ultimately fell back on my law enforcement training and simply attempted to create an environment where Jodie Evans could tell her truth to the American people. I think to a greater degree this happened and the results should be looked at long and hard by Americans who love the military and this country.

In my humble opinion, based upon my conversation with Jodie Evans, she is most definitely a communist sympathizer and carries strong anti-American sentiment. She combines the dangerous combination of the naiveté that communist dictators troll for when looking for dupes to spread their propaganda with the zealousness of the extremists we see around the world. In short, Evans may very well be a fool, but she's a fool who truly believes in what she is doing and this is the most chilling thing of all. Evans' statements in her interview on the Conscience of Kansas radio program are radical and they enrage those who love this country.

On a larger scope, Evans' statements on the Conscience of Kansas radio program should validate the conservatives who have come before me and reported the communistic nature of Jodie Evans and the anti-American stance brought forward by the leadership of Code Pink. The only difference now is that the transition from pink to red; that is, communist red, can now be taken directly from the lips of Jodie Evans. (Ibbetson, 2008, June 18)

Of course, embedding video in articles and columns was not just part of exposing liberal fanatics. I also incorporated them in illuminating American comebacks such as in the Duane "Dog" Chapman interview. Duane Chapman was my guest on the eve of his July 16, 2008, television comeback. The video links to the program are: http://www.youtube.com/watch?v=GBHBOMSW1JU and http://www.youtube.com/watch?v=qFBbSzoA-lk. The following article on Chapman was published around the net and was picked up by the official Duane Dog Chapman Website.

Perseverance: Reflections from a Conversation with Duane "Dog" Chapman

On June 24, 2008, I had a lengthy interview with Duane "Dog" Chapman. Chapman is the star of A&E's returning hit show *Bounty Hunter*, where he will once again track felons on the run before a nation of thrilled television viewers. Chapman was gracious enough to take a break from what will be season number five of the *Bounty Hunter* program to talk with me on my radio show the "Conscience of Kansas." I think the interview had many exciting facets, and I invite readers to watch both part one and part two of the YouTube version of our conversation. What I would like to focus my discussion on today is my own reflections on the controversy surrounding the man known as "Dog" Chapman.

Currently, Chapman is attempting a comeback of not only his television program but also a resurrection of his name in the public eye following the racist comments that came to national attention back in November 2007. It is here that those who wish to look beyond the flamboyant tough guy presentation that Chapman exudes can see, if they wish, a bit of character which is often lacking in many individuals whose reputations have not suffered the verbal bashing that Chapman has endured over the past several months. There are no apologies here for Chapman; his words in a private conversation with a family member that were made public were hurtful to many and rightly so. However, while we should not minimize the damaging impact of Chapman's words, I believe it would also be folly to forget how he handled a situation that threatened both his career and personal name. In an environment today that promotes victimization and the avoidance of accountability, Chapman placed the fault of his statements where many politicians will not; that is, he took the blame head on.

Having apologized in almost every venue possible, Chapman steps back into the public eye in hopes of renewing his former stardom. The question is, will the nation embrace him as before? Some people may refuse to forgive the audio clips of Chapman's derogatory private statements from 2007; others may remember the man that courageously nabbed the serial rapist Andrew Luster in Mexico, which most certainly saved other women from the most egregious of personal violations. What I observed from my conversation with the man called "Dog" was a unique mixture of the goodness and imperfection that is in all of us. Specifically, Duane Chapman is gregarious but gracious, gruff but extremely kind; he is blunt while also being very articulate.

In short, there are many facets to this individual that the camera may not readily capture. The most notable of these characteristics that caught my eye is that Chapman has a genuineness about him that becomes apparent when discussing his life passion in bounty hunting. Chapman appears to not only understand the dangers involved in dealing with the individuals he tracks, but he also appears to empathize with those same individuals, who due to their life choices, have found themselves with the "Dog" on their heels.

Will Duane "Dog" Chapman reclaim his former popularity? Only the future will tell. However, if I were a betting man, I would say that the odds are in Chapman's favor as folks tend to gravitate toward people they see as authentic, despite their imperfections. Americans, by their nature, also have an undeniable attraction to those who embody the American Spirit — to pick themselves up out of the dirt without complaints or excuses, dust themselves off, and keep on doing their best. I call this tenacity to overcome life's hurdles perseverance. Duane Chapman terms it simply as "hanging in there." Either way, it's one of the components of success, and you can bet that the man named "Dog" is tracking a full comeback with the same effort he puts into every manhunt. As for me, I hope he finds it. (Ibbetson, 2008, June 30)

I share my journey in radio as it is germane to my overall growth as a conservative and it is an example of how I implement the conservative philosophy that has been the focus of this book. In early 2008, the *Conscience of Kansas* radio program was awarded the entertainment program of the year for graduate student radio by the Kansas Association of Broadcasters. It was a wonderful feeling to be recognized for all the hard work. Personally, I have found something special in radio and I place great focus on it in my future. With that said, I could not have moved forward in the radio arena without observing the conservative principles brought forth in Chapter 4, i.e. (1) God, (2) Family, and (3) Country. It's still the same superior conservative principles that drive success, whether it's in becoming a nationally recognized radio host, a person who gets out to vote, or just someone who has the motivation to speak up when something needs to be said. It's all important stuff and the part that each individual plays in the conservative quest to save this country is of the upmost importance now!

References

Ibbetson, P. A. (2008, June 18). From pink to red. *World Net Daily*. Retrieved from http://www.worldnetdaily.com/index.php/index.php/index.php?fa=PAGE.view&pageId=67228

Ibbetson, P. A. (2008, June 30). Perseverance: Reflections from a conversation with Duane "Dog" Chapman. *Renew America*. Retrieved from http://www.renewamerica.us/columns/ibbetson/080630

Chapter 10

<hr>

Zoo You Believe?

SO BY THIS POINT I hope you can see that the issues conservatives face today are serious; that the battle to defeat political correctness and the evasive liberal culture is a battle we can lose or win. This is a good thing but also scary at the same time. The future of this country is in our hands. This puts all the responsibility on our shoulders, which is a little scary, but I am optimistic. Why? Because at its core, when you peel away the fringe, this is a nation that champions conservative values. The United States still embodies a national conscience that recognizes its blessings come from God and a need to uphold the traditional values of the founding fathers who looked for divine guidance when creating this country. Greatness has never, and will never, be an entitlement; it is something that comes from standing up and helping yourself and helping others. When I want examples of what still makes America great, I look to home, the people of Kansas. In Kansas, like every state in the nation, when the going gets tough people still come together. This article shows the American spirit at its best when it has to be — the worst of times.

Greensburg, Kansas: When the Tornado Veers Left

On April 19, 2000, a storm gathered on a summer evening in Kansas. Not so unusual an event, nor the tornado watches that accompany so many summer days here in tornado alley. Having lived here since birth, I can tell you that tornados are a seasonal part of life and children are taught in early grade school what to do when the alarms sound. Parents learn early, as well, that the value of a good neighbor is only trumped by the value of a good neighbor with a sturdy basement. Despite the preparation and respect that Kansans carry for this black swirling beast, it is easy to forget the full extent of the dangers that they bring. Why? Because so often the tornado veers right; that is, most often our tornadoes form and work their way through the isolated plains wreaking no more damage than displacing a farmer's barn or aggravating the cows and their evening supper. Unfortunately, this is not always the case.

On April 19, 2000, I saw the viciousness and power of the tornado up close. As is often the case in Kansas, despite the technological advances to tornado warning systems, when the threat is near, storm watchers are sprinkled across the countryside near the communities at risk. Law enforcement, among others, often fills the duty as temporary sentinels of the plains. Dutifully, we patrol our little areas of beautiful Kansas and send word at the first sign of danger. It was in this capacity that I watched a tornado, a big one, a town killer, form before me. I was transfixed, if not mesmerized, as I watched the black eerie swirling winds give birth to a growing funnel that reached down to the earth and began ripping apart everything in its path. I could hear the freight train shrill of the tornado and it's a sound that one should go a lifetime without hearing. However, on this evening for the little town of Cherryvale, Kansas, the town of which I served and lived, the tornado veered right. That is, it wove around the city limits and, in a moment, disappeared to the east. While Cherryvale was spared, the tornado showed no mercy to the neighboring town of Parsons, Kansas. It was then I learned a valuable lesson. Sometimes the tornado veers left and goes straight down your throat with the power to take property, livelihoods, and even precious life. Walking through the town of Parsons, people were in a state of shock, becoming literally lost on streets they had walked for years as lifelong markers had been removed in the massive damage to the city. If it is fair to say that the Parsons, Kansas, tornado brought calamity, the tornado in Greensburg brought utter catastrophe. Seeing the total destruction in Greensburg is the visual equivalent of a World War II bombing photo. Yes, the tornado veered left, big time.

To the inhabitants of the 1,500 people who called this town their home, the Greensburg that they knew is gone, but I hazard to think that Greensburg may not be done. I say this with no intention of creating a feel good article as I believe that nothing can take away the loss the people of Greensburg feel at this time. However, I do observe the same American spirit in Greensburg that I saw in Parsons years ago. A spirit of mourning and consoling, mixed with an optimistic determinism that only comes from a reliance on God. People from around the state, as well as the nation, brought forth aid and support, both in prayer and funds, that Parsons would survive. This assistance is now extended to Greensburg that they might recover as best as possible. I am always tempted to see this selflessness and self sacrifice as a unique Kansas quality as I see it here in action so often; but in reality, it's an American quality. It's reflected in the generosity after natural disasters such as those seen in Florida, New Orleans, and the list goes on and on. Americans, with all our limitations, come forth time and time again to help those in need. It's what we do; it's an American quality worth fighting for, as well as observing in the direct aftermath of the storm. Today it's Greensburg, and no one knows where the dark clouds will form tomorrow. What I do believe is that through the wondrous power of God, the American spirit prevails, and with that spirit, Parsons survived, and surely so will Greensburg. This has been a humble observation of the American spirit so wonderfully displayed in Greensburg, Kansas, days after the tornado veered left. (Ibbetson, 2007, May 18)

Life is like a trip to the zoo. We started with this unique saying and it seems only fitting to conclude with the same. We have taken a long journey together through many articles that attempt to stand up for my conservative beliefs, beliefs I feel are shared by the majority of the nation. Notice I did not say a vocal majority. That's one of the problems our majority faces. With this book I am not pretending to attempt a formalized movement. Instead, I am trying to stimulate people to think about where they stand on the issues and to discover the hidden conservative within them. If this dormant conservative political characteristic is realized within the U.S. populace, the wondrous potential for good is endless. Conversely, if America continues to inch along toward the socialistic end goals of liberalism, we will someday face a terrible day of reckoning. Those days may be fewer in number than you think.

When I think of a Barack Hussein Obama presidency, I can only see socialism and its big brother, communism, finding its way into more niches within this country. Not everyone will agree with my thoughts about the political world and some will get confused and even mad with every page they turn. I am not unaccustomed to these reactions. Spending as many years as I have in the halls of academia has been a lot like opening day of the exotic exhibit at the zoo. You know, the first day when they bring out the strange foreign creature from an unknown land and they don't have a name plate that describes that animal up yet? People look in wonder at the animal that appears to come from another world, "are those feathers or flippers; teeth or a beak?" Spectator and animal stare at one another in curious wonderment with nothing in common and no idea how to figure each other out. Situations like that are often just another day in academia to me. A conservative in the land of the liberals. Fortunately, I believe that I have been able to take the best from the college experience and leave the propaganda behind. In short, I think I will leave with my soul. One of the best defenses I have had to liberalism is the ability to laugh off the nonsense and never let it get me down. A daily injection of humor just seems to help encourage a general feeling of optimism. So it seems only fitting to leave you a humorous article that looks at those silly liberal Democrats from a Kansas country boy perspective. Life is like a trip to the zoo and, for me, the first zoo I got to see was for free, right there on the farm. Feel free to laugh.

You See it All on the Farm

If you want to see some interesting and often humorous similarities in life, just take a trip to the farm. Having lived a great portion of my life in the country, I see parallels to all aspects of politics that play out daily in the pastures, fields, and woods of Kansas. Let me share with you a few humorous country analogues, that I believe, at least my fellow brothers and sisters of the soil will be able to identify with.

I have been amused for some time with the Democrats pick of Howard Dean as the Chairman of the Democratic National Committee. Few can argue, though at times I think some level-headed Democrats try, that the Chairman of the Democratic National Committee represents the face of the party to the world. Every time I watch Mr. Dean speak I have had the funny feeling that something is familiar about the man. Something I've seen before, but from where? After lengthy contemplation, it came to me; yes, it's something you see on the farm. For Mr. Dean, it's all in the eyes and something I used to see in the cattle on the farm. You know, when the storm comes rolling in and the herd becomes agitated and for the most part unreliable. You can see that look in the cow's eye, when a little too much white is visible above and below the pupil. When you see it you know it and you give the cattle a lot of space on that day, because in that particular state, they are not just a danger to themselves, but to you as well. Farmers have an uncanny sense of such things but it's a little more elusive when watching it on the television. I recommend you test my observation and watch a little footage of the DNC Chairman for simple humor value sometime. You see it whether the Chairman is besmirching a minority group or ranting his way through a list of the states in the union. Even in the calmest of times, DNC Chairman Dean has that look, that special little twinkle in the eye that unequivocally says, "Yes, I'm crazy." We laugh because it's funny; we laugh a little harder when we know it's true. It's not just the look itself but also the fact that it always silently signals an unknown and radical action that no one can foretell. When Chairman Dean steps up to the microphone it's like a giant roulette wheel has been spun. Will he say something poignant today or will he light himself on fire and jump into the crowd? Your guess is as good as mine. I have affectionately coined the look "Howard Dean wild-eyed;" something tells me this has the potential to become a household term. So for you farm folk, the next time the bull has spent the morning playing with the bumblebees, be kind enough to tell the neighbor that you share fences with that "el torro" has a mighty case of "Howard Dean wild-eye" today, it's what good neighbors do.

Yes my friends, you see it all on the farm. It does not take long to find the farmyard animal that represents the Democratic Party as a whole. Now hold on! If you think that the donkey wins automatically you're mistaken. In fact, I think that this beast of burden kinda gets a bum rap. I know that there are certain similarities that are shared, such as an uncanny stubbornness in times when cooperation is a necessity. However, when the donkey puts its mind too it, what little mind there is, it can get a lot done. In short, the donkey just doesn't fit the bill. When you're looking for which animal most closely represents the Democratic Party, it has to be the turkey. Yes, from birth to death the turkey is pure Democrat. Let me explain. Like the Democrats of today, the turkey lives in its own specific reality. From birth, the turkey has an uncanny way of getting itself into predicaments. Self-preservation is just not one of its strong suits. If it rains in the corner of the pen, the turkey dutifully walks over to the corner and drowns. If the turkey can get its head through the fencing, it hangs itself by morning. In fact, the early life of the turkey is often extended by the fact that the other critters of the farm often block the turkey from being able to get to its destination where its inability to cope with daily life would at some point overwhelm it and cause the turkey's certain demise.

When the turkey becomes an adult the comparison is even more evident. Like the Democratic Party, the turkey tries to run the entire farm. Challenging the rooster at day break for vocal supremacy, the turkey yells his way through the entire day. That piercing boom of "gobble gobble!" which translates in human to "reporting for duty!" is combined with the narcissistic inflation of the body and the turkey is ready to patrol his ground. Like our friends from the left, the turkey can pull off the tough guy routine for only short stints. With a face three shades redder than Ted Kennedy, the turkey literally shakes with authority. He will even give you a little flogging if you show him your backside at the wrong time. However, when faced with a truly formidable foe, the turkey quickly deflates and shows the barnyard assembly the true meaning of cut and run. We certainly don't hate the turkey as he makes life on the farm very interesting; however, both man and beast alike understand that the turkey can never be allowed to run the show. In fact, like the Democrat Party, no matter how much latitude is given to the turkey to strut and gobble, it's best if they're eaten for lunch every two to four years.

As you return back to your daily lives, which for many are far from the gravel roads where the lessons of the country begin, remember this: There's a little bit of country in Washington politics, but if you look hard enough, there's a whole lot of Washington politics in the country. The trick is to keep your eyes open. Give it a shot sometime and you'll soon agree, you see it all on the farm. (Ibbetson, 2006, October 17)

References

Ibbetson, P. A. (2007, May 18). Greensburg, Kansas: When the tornado veers left. *The Conservative Voice*. Retrieved from http://www.the-conservativevoice.com/article/25461.html

Ibbetson, P. A. (2006, October 17). You see it all on the farm. *The Land of the Free*. Retrieved from http://www.thelandofthefree.net/con-servativeopinion/2006/10/17/you-see-it-all-on-the-farm/

APPENDIX "A"

Reader Mail -- Supporting Views

I can never thank readers enough for sending in 'letters to the editor' for all the websites I write for. Sending an e-mail takes time and I have learned that they are worth not only reading but sharing with others. I have always read every e-mail or letter sent to me; however, early on I did not save the e-mails as I thought I would not have a use for them. I regret that and I now share a few of the reader responses to my articles and the websites from which they came. Let's start with the kind letters of support and then move on to the folks (liberals) who had some other ideas and recommendations for me.

Seven Minutes of Limbaugh

Reader response in the "Howard Was Right" Journal http://howard-wasright.com

Paul-

Well written article on Rush.

I had a strong distaste for the man up until about 1998, when my then father-in-law reset me a bit. I have a sense of humor, and I am not dumb, but I never got Rush's keen use of hyperbole for effect, and until someone who knew better helped me see it, the intent was lost, and all I heard was the delivery.

I can now sum up your article with seven words: Try to prove that Rush is wrong.

If you really look at what he says objectively, you will quickly find that his seeming 'braggadocios' style is for effect, and that he is indeed right, 98.6% of the time -- or whatever the current running ratio is! :-)

Bravo from fly-over country.

Reader response in the "Canada Free Press" http://www.canadafree-press.com/

What a fine tribute to a man that has made such a vast change in today's political climate. I will attempt to forward your excellent article on to Rush. The fact that you have labored in the bowels of academe as a Conservative, is remarkable. It must have been lonely for you there.

Reader response in the "Canada Free Press" http://www.canadafree-press.com/

Mr. Ibbetson,

I want to keep this short as I know you are busy, but as a Rush fan you will find it interesting. In the Fall of 1993 I came home to the Seattle area from an overseas job in Singapore. I had been away for three years working as a pilot for Singapore Airlines. I had read things about Rush during my absence, but knew very little about him, basically just knew he was a conservative radio host. We arrived home during the first week of school, so we were rushing around, getting settled into our old home, and the most importantly getting the three youngest of our six boys enrolled and off to school every day. I was the morning driver, and on the second day I heard this voice on the radio, political, conservative, amusing, Rush of course. I was immediately hooked. When I arrived home I told my wife, "I just heard this guy Rush Limbaugh, he really is good. My wife, who had never been political, had never heard him either, but said, "I hate that man, Sandy (her liberal friend) says he is a right wing bigot", end of conversation. So each morning I would tune up KVI here in Seattle, drive the kids to school and come home. My wife would take the car, run her errands, tune up her favorite radio station, and return. So it went for several weeks until I noticed that every morning the radio was still tuned to KVI. Could it be? I asked my wife, "are you listening to Rush Limbaugh"? She was hooked, now more conservative than I am, if that is possible. I thought you might enjoy this little episode.

Reader response in the "Canada Free Press" http://www.canadafree-press.com/

Great article on Rush Limbaugh, beautifully written. We have been fans of Rush for many years. Hope is gets into the America Press.

Reader response in the "Canada Free Press" http://www.canadafree-press.com/

Enjoyed (and agreed with) your article re: Rush Limbaugh. Delighted to learn you're a Kansan!

Welcome back anytime. We could use you.

Reader response in the "Canada Free Press" http://www.canadafree-press.com/

Dittos to you brother!!

Reader response in the "Canada Free Press" http://www.canadafree-press.com/

Dear Mr. Ibbetson,

Great read for my Friday morning.

From The Pew to the Pulpit: Inside the Church of Global Warming

Reader response in the "Canada Free Press" http://www.canadafree-press.com/

If you really want to look under the alarm at the science it's not so alarming. CO_2 is the third most abundant natural greenhouse gas. Water vapor and methane are more important than CO_2 and water vapor is far more abundant. A recent study by Ernst-Georg Beck shows that the ICPP CO_2 data were wrong. CO_2 was higher in 1942 when it reached 400 pm. CO_2 is soluble in the oceans so that warming causes CO_2 to bubble off. Cooling allows absorption. CO2 is not the cause; it has been shown to be a trailing effect of natural cooling and warming. The best measurements show 0.55 to 0.7 increases globally over the past 100 years or so. The land stations are corrupt and there are few marine weather stations. There is, however, a 95% correlation between solar activity and lack of it. That science comes from the Danish National Space Center over the past 25 years. Solar activity induces (raises) the earth's magnetic shield; cosmic radiation from deep space, the Milky Way and the sun cause clouds on earth and cooling when the geomagnetic shield is down. If you live in a humid place on the planet, you may have had cloudy weather since last October as we entered a sunspot cycle minimum and the shields are now down and cosmic radiation is penetrating and causing cloud formation. During the normal sunspot cycle the shield is up, fewer clouds form and warming occurs. There is 5% left, plus or minus, for anthropocentric warming except that some scientists have concluded that the CO2 greenhouse effect is non-linear and vanishingly small at the current level. These earth, solar system, galaxy-wide systems are immense. It is the height of narcissism to think mankind is having an impact. Moreover, The UN has never allowed the solar evidence to be discussed in the ICPP reports. It's all about us - it's a product of narcissistic new age 'religion'. We might as well offer incense to stop plate tectonics and continental drift.

Reader response in the "Canada Free Press" http://www.canadafree-press.com/

There is no question that the Kyoto treaty was a waste. It was either too little to do any good or it was stifling to the world's economy. Amazing when a treaty can do two things bad. I discuss this on my site http://www.globalwarming-factorfiction.com.

Reader response in the "Iain Hall Blogspot" http://iainhall.wordpress.com/

I am not the only person who thinks that the whole global warming thing is a new secular religion. The piece I quote below makes the same case with a particular emphasis on this faith's self styled Pope Al Gore. This piece makes some good points about populism vs empirical facts the former being the driver of this "debate" in the absence of enough of the latter to actually do as the AGW proponents claim; to prove beyond any doubt that it is the activity of humanity that is driving the perceived changes in the worlds weather.

Reader mail from the "Conservative Voice" http://www.theconserva-tivevoice.com/

Gore, poster boy for liberalism, is the sickening example of incompetence and hypocrisy if not stupidity, making or trying to make rules for everybody else to follow.

Reader mail from the "Conservative Voice" http://www.theconserva-tivevoice.com/

Thank you Paul for your great commentary.

My younger brother (I now have 3 brothers, used to have 4) the scientist, a doctor of Physics, agrees totally with your doubts about man-caused, global warming, and he`s not only into physics, but also optics,(concerning abm targetting systems),advanced propulsion, astronomy, weather forecasting by the sunspots, antigravity propulsion, oceanography, geology, advanced mathematics, etc: a well-rounded scientist, wouldn`t you say? Anyway, I've asked him if he would write a commentary for TCV in this newsletter, debunking global warming (man-caused).

Michael Moore: A Criminal Profile

Reader mail from the "New Media Journal" http://www.therant.us/

All your points on Moore are valid. There was a time in this country when he would have been so marginalized that he never would have stuck his head out the door again. His hypocrisy is off the charts and his list of stra nge bedfellows looks like the top 10 Who's Who list of the Communist party. I think the key is to marginalize the production by marshalling the prominent voices of various industries including Hollywood, big business, ethnic affiliations, lobbyist, academics and centrist politicians on both sides of the aisle. Intellectually arguing and countering Moore's productions are not too difficult. Proving he is a liar only requires equal media coverage from those voices that have influence and credibility. Then I believe they can put Michael Moore's propaganda to rest at least until George Soros bankrolls his next production as he has with Air America and other disastrous media outlets. Keep fighting the good fight. Good luck on your Doctorate Degree!

Editor from "First Friday Collective" at http://firstfriday.wordpress.com/2007/06/06/

Rare is it that we here at the First Friday blog will post something completely unoriginal, but every once in a while we come across something so true and well done that we have to post it in the hope of getting as many eyes on it as possible.

We will have much more to say about Jabba the Commie in the coming weeks, but this is about as good as it gets when it comes to exposing him for what he is.

Reader from "First Friday Collective" at http://firstfriday.wordpress.com/2007/06/06/

Amen, Paul. Amen.

The Value of Anger

Reader mail from the "Conservative Voice" http://www.theconservativevoice.com/

Any criticism of the US, if done in a well intentioned, thoughtful manner, is always welcomed. The problem is the communist/liberals don't start or stop with well intentioned criticism. A perfect example of the lefts true goals, traits, and methods is the NY Times; treason by any other name should still get the entire staff the death sentence. As far as Bush being an idiot, well I don't know how smart he is or is not, but what was our other choice? Gore? Kerry? And you want to claim we are in bad shape now? We would be bowing down to our new Muslim masters if either one of those spineless simpletons were in office. And if that were not enough, and if for no other reason, the Supreme Court nominations could not be left to the liberal/communists. The agenda that the Liberals have not been able to implement via the Congress (the entire liberal agenda) has been forced on the American people via black robed criminals in the Supreme Court.

Reader mail from the "Conservative Voice" http://www.theconserva-tivevoice.com

Anger is an emotion, something we all feel from time to time. Anger is not good or bad, what we do with it is either appropriate, or inappropriate. We cannot go through life pleasing mommy and daddy in our subconscious. We must eventually grow up, and accept responsibility for our actions. My last experience with liberals reminded me of why I'm conservative. THEY were the ones who spewed anger regarding politics, and religion. Both of which THEY brought into an otherwise nice chat. Anyway, as long as we channel anger constructively as in the immigration fiasco as of late, there's nothing wrong with anger.

Reader mail from the "New Media Journal" http://www.therant.us/

Thank you, Paul!

A good portion of the frustration that I've struggled with for the last year or two has come from encounters with people - including loved ones - who have admonished me against "getting angry" over what I see happening to our nation. Their view is that anger is an "evil", useless, and destructive emotion that a "real" Christian should never, ever feel under any circumstances.

Needless to say, I disagree with every fiber of my being. As you pointed out in your article, Jesus himself acted in anger by physically throwing the money-changers out of the Temple. And the Bible says that God made us in HIS image, so I believe we are programmed to experience that same "righteous anger" when we witness Evil happening.

And watching our own elected representatives sell out this nation that God established - exposing all of our citizens to the hardships of a wrecked economy and society, and the horrors of Islamic terrorism - fills me with that same anger. It's wrong. It's evil. And it needs to be stopped. And I don't care whose political toes get stepped on, or whose "sensitivity" gets offended. This isn't some entertaining "debate" at the local Ladies' Garden Society - our very survival as a nation is at stake.

Please keep putting out this message.

Reader mail from the "New Media Journal" http://www.therant.us/

The American People are descended from the Cream of the Crop that the world had to offer. Only the very tough, courageous, smart and capable even attempted a months-long ocean voyage on a wooden sailing ship to reach a wild, unsettled land. Only the healthiest, toughest and most capable of THOSE survived once they arrived in the New World - because there certainly weren't any Social Services offices waiting to "meet their needs". And even the slaves, brought here against their will - were "culled" by hardship so that only the healthiest, toughest and most capable among them survived the scourge of Slavery.

We, the People, can save our nation if we just remember who we are - and get angry over the Evil being to our nation by enemies both foreign and domestic. And if we stand up and refuse to allow this to happen - if we stand for what is Right and Good - I believe that God will give us Victory again, just as He gave it to an out-numbered, out-gunned, out-strategized bunch of colonists 231 years ago.

But first, we need to get angry - and we have every right to be.

God bless and keep you and yours - and God preserve America.

AUTHOR'S NOTE: It is impossible to say how important it is to get encouraging words from readers. There is plenty of opposition out there and sharing the conservative philosophy is truly like *Feeding Lions*; however, a kind word goes a long way in helping the brave fight the good fight.

Now we take a look at some of the readers who had opposing views. It's not only fair to share liberal opinions, it's also very educational. Like I said before, when a person places their time and effort to create an e-mail, they are truly motivated and often they show a true glimpse of themselves.

Reader Mail -- Opposing Views

Why Democrats Fear The Patriot Act

Editor of the "Patriot Act News" at http://patriotactnews.blogspot. com/2006/01/democrats-fear-patriot-act.html

According to an opinion piece in The American Daily by Paul Ibbetson, Democrats fear (not hate nor dislike) the Patriot Act.

Ibbetson has a theory as to why Democrats dislike the Act:

1) He suggests that Democrats have been unable to think or devise an alternative strategies for the War on Terror

2) and that the Act itself represents action

While this theory may apply to some liberals out there, I think we have seen that most Democrats in Congress support most of the Act. In question and up for debate are those provisions that may or may not violate civil liberties.

I think it is dangerous to say that just debating or questioning the Act means you are against stopping terrorists. This country has a long history of debate and free speech. These are the last things we should be willing to let go of.

From The Pew to the Pulpit: Inside the Church of Global Warming

Reader response in the "Iain Hall Blogspot" http://iainhall.word-press.com/

I do agree some people are using the AGW debate to further their careers; Al Gore is a good example. I know some environmentalists who do place religious overlays on their work which is not that strange (they believe the earth has a spirit). I'm an atheist, but I except that others have spiritual or religious beliefs, it's their journey.

The post by Paul A. Ibbetson is just gutter rubbish and typical of the extreme right.

His best point against Gore is that he is a "portly prophet of doomsday prognostications". Wow so he's fat. His argument must be crap then.

As for the hysteria about his 'footprint' I think one of Gore's own people said it best;

"I think what you're seeing here is the last gasp of the global warming skeptics. They've completely lost the debate on the issue so now they're just attacking their most effective opponent."

As for comparing all environmentalists and climate scientists with Jim Jones, well words fail me. The best I can call his ranting is utter crap.

Michael Moore: A Criminal Profile

Reader mail from the "Conservative Voice" http://www.theconserva-tivevoice.com/

Michael Moore doesn't appear "anti-American". Anti-republican maybe, but not anti-American. Insulting republicans is not the same as hating your country. Insulting the president is not the same thing as hating your country. Even hating republicans is not the same as hating America. The republicans would have us believe that if you insult, ridicule, or hate the way the politicians run the country - you hate America. Nice try, republicans.

Reader mail from the "Conservative Voice" http://www.theconserva-tivevoice.com/

If you read this carefully including the promotion of the author and his book, you should be able to see that he fits his own definition of a sociopath. I am sure he doesn't realize it, because "crazy" people don't know their crazy. I also sense some paranoia and obsessive tendencies with this author in regards to Mr. Moore. I don't believe everything Mr. Moore says, or for that matter anybody, but his movies do offer insights into other points of view. These points of view are critical to understanding this issue that is being discussed. I don't think Michael Moore is harmful to anybody, because people, most of them, are able to realize that his movies represent his opinions, whether backed by lies or not. This author seems to believe that people don't realize this and that he must save us from ourselves and Mr. Moore by comparing Mr. Moore to a sociopath. Simply put Mr. Moore is a person who makes movies about controversial topics. In these movies he promotes his opinions using shock, cut and paste editing to give only portions of truth and other techniques to satisfy his need to persuade people to see his point of view at the same time selling his movie. This author clearly does the same. He is selling a book, right? Don't politicians, advertisers, preachers and just people in everyday situations do the same? Are we all sociopaths? Don't anybody answer that!

Reader from "First Friday Collective" at http://firstfriday.wordpress.com/2007/06/06/

Funny…to align yourselves with the hard-christian white might, and then quote Chris Hitchens…that's funny. Should someone be pointing out America's shortcomings make them Anti-American, is like saying you have a huge…well you know. The comparisons to Bundy are weak, and show not creative thought within a methodically written talking point that might as well have been created in a creative writing class. I once knew a plump loudmouth from Michigan, who spewed right-wing talking points as far back as I knew him. If I were to say his actions and words were comparable to un-patriotic during the Clinton era or that living liberally in that span he would have been offended. The fact that you use Michael Moore as a target shows how bad your righties aim is…he's so big you couldn't miss! The left will use their reality of a filmmakers word, and the right will use a book that professes differently. I also find it funny that a bunch of righties who hate Hollywood would embrace Fred Thompson, does he mean it, or is he acting? This could also be seen as personal gain…correct? Fred Thompson inc. so to speak…Now watch this drive!!!!

Reader from "First Friday Collective" at http://firstfriday.wordpress.com/2007/06/06/

How the f%*$ did the author of the article, or us, align ourselves with the Christian f&*$#%g "White" whatever that is? Jesus Christ, you missed the point on this one, yo.

The Value of Anger

Reader mail from the "Conservative Voice" http://www.theconservativevoice.com/

This is such a common theme in the arguments of those who blog on TCV. Equating "America" with the politicians who run the country. There is absolutely nothing wrong with hating the way our leaders have run the country. It doesn't mean you "hate America" because our leaders are not America. Can any conservatives give an honest reason as to why so many of their compatriots are quick to equate criticism of the U.S. foreign policy practiced by our leaders to "hating America?"

APPENDIX "B"

Conservative Website Directory

To this day I still search the internet every week for new and exciting conservative websites. Its tough, time consuming work, but the rewards of new intellectually stimulating writers and news sources are always worth the search. In creating a conservative website directory for readers, I hope that I can cut a little bit of that research time down for the next person, and it is also a way for me to say "thank you" for the websites that publish my columns and those who have given me wonderful insights into the conservative movement worldwide. I recommend that you look at every one of these websites as they each have a uniqueness and their own special knowledge of conservatism waiting to be found by the eager researcher.

The American Conservative Worker:
http://michaelwestfall.tripod.com/

American Dailey: http://americandaily.com/

American Patriots For True Equality (APFTE): http://www.apfte.net/

The American Prophet: http://americanprophet.org/

Americans For Legal Immigration: http://www.alipac.us/

American Thinker: http://www.americanthinker.com/

Capitol Hill Coffee House: http://capitolhillcoffeehouse.com/

ChronWatch: http://www.chronwatch-america.com/

The Common Sense Conservative: http://www.greatamericanjournal.com/

The Conservative Crusader: www.conservativecrusader.com/

The Conservative Voice: http://www.theconservativevoice.com/

Erik Rush: http://erikrush.com/

Faith Freedom International: http://www.faithfreedom.org/

The First Friday Collective: http://firstfriday.wordpress.com/

The Free Republic: http://www.freerepublic.com/

FrontPage Magazine: http://www.frontpagemag.com/

GOPUSA: http://www.gopusa.com/

Great American Journal: http://www.greatamericanjournal.com/

The Hill Chronicles: http://thehillchronicles.com/

Howard Was Right: http://howardwasright.com/

Immigration Watch Dog: http://www.immigrationwatchdog.com/

The Intellectual Conservative: http://intellectualconservative.com/

Jihad Watch: http://jihadwatch.org/

The Jim Gilchrist Official Website: http://jimgilchrist.com/blog/

The Land of the Free: http://www.thelandofthefree.net

Made in the USA: http://www.argonunya.com/madeinusa.html

The Minuteman Project: http://www.minutemanproject.com/

MichNews: http://www.michnews.com/

Military Magazine: www.milmag.com/

The MoveOff Network: http://moveoff.net/

New Media Journal: http://www.therant.us/

News By Us: http://newsbyus.com/

The Political Nightmare: http://www.politicalnightmare.com/

The Post Chronicle: http://www.postchronicle.com/

The Reality Check: http://www.therealitycheck.org/

The Religion of Peace: http://www.thereligionofpeace.com/

Renew America: http://www.renewamerica.us/

Republican and Proud: http://www.republicanandproud.com/

Republican Voices: http://republicanvoices.org/

The View From 1776: http://www.thomasbrewton.com/index.php

Web Today: http://www.888webtoday.com/

The Yankee Commentary: http://www.yankeecommentary.blogspot.com/

APPENDIX "C"

Conservative Radio Directory

Radio is one of the most powerful communication mediums in the country. It's only fitting that conservatives have absolute rule here when it comes to political talk shows. The following directory will include some of my favorite shows on the radio and internet with URL's to enable readers to check them out and make up their own minds on who they like best. I will include a short narrative about programs that I have been on as a guest to give readers as complete a feel for these unique educational and inspirational radio programs.

The Rush Limbaugh Program: http://www.rushlimbaugh.com/

There is probably no one as funny or creative as Rush Limbaugh. From the comical music parodies by Paul Shanklin, to the daily denouncing of global warming, Rush Limbaugh is the undisputed champion of conservative talk radio.

The Sean Hannity Show: http://www.hannity.com/

Sean Hannity is one of the top five conservative radio hosts in the country. He never backs down from a fight and his program is full of entertaining guests and topics. Hannity's "man on the street" segment often opens the eyes of radio listeners when the general public is tapped for their knowledge of politics.

The Glenn Beck Program: http://www.glennbeck.com/

The Glenn Beck Program is another of the five most popular conservative radio programs in the country. Beck has a quick wit, and with his side kick "Stu," they make an entertaining program. I believe that his constant attack on the validity of manmade global warming is one of the facets of his show I like best.

The Radio Factor with Bill O'Reilly: *http://www.billoreilly.com/site*

The Radio Factor is an entertaining show. Bill O'Reilly may be one of the most aggressive radio hosts on the dial and he is known to shout and call people (pinheads). O'Reilly is an activist radio host and I found his work to "Boycott France" very amusing. I also found his work on "Jessica's Law," a law to increase the penalties for sexual offenders, to be as brilliant an endeavor as it was noble. I don't agree with O'Reilly's stance on manmade global warming and the death penalty, to name a few issues; however, he's a free thinker with a strong backbone, not afraid to fight the liberal left, and I find myself listening and agreeing with him a lot.

The Savage Nation: *http://prosites-prs.homestead.com/index.html*

Michael Savage is one of the outsiders of conservative talk radio. A former liberal turned conservative, the highly educated Savage can rail at liberals with a ferocity that is unmatched in the radio world. Known for his over the top statements, Savage enjoys a large loyal listenership. I could never say I agree with everything Savage utters on the radio; however, he does say a lot of things I wish I could say but don't.

The Neal Boortz Show: *http://boortz.com/*

Neal Boortz is a very interesting character. He is the co-author with John Linder of the "Fair Tax Book" which relevance still places it in pertinent debates today. Boortz is a no-nonsense radio host who often hangs up on his guests if they ruffle his feathers. Boortz is a Libertarian and he often shares conversions with co-producers Royal Marshall and Belinda Skelton on the air.

The Tammy Bruce Show: *http://tammybruce.com/*

Tammy Bruce is a true anomaly. Bruce is an openly gay, pro-gun, pro-life, pro-death penalty radio host. She is a former liberal activist who became a conservative radio host. Go figure. Bruce is obviously brilliant and you will know that if you read any of her books. I admit, with her past resume, I was slow to be a listener and I don't agree with everything she says. What her program does show, however, is the interesting diversity of those who fall under the conservative tent.

The Flip Side Show with Don Crawford: http://www.flipsideshow. com/

Don Crawford was the first radio host to have a show aired by Armed Forces Radio Network. Don was kind enough to allow me on his radio program where we had a stimulating discussion on the Patriot Act. The Flip Side has many interesting guests and I recommend it to those wanting to hear another great conservative at work.

Stand Up America: http://www.ospreymedia.us/wordpress/

Stand Up America is aired through OSPREY Radio and is hosted by Paul Vallely, Major U.S. Army General retired. Vallely is a military FOX News contributor. I was honored to be able to spend a few moments on June 11, 2007, with the General and talk about the effects of the Patriot Act. Later, General Vallely was kind enough to allow the posting of my article, *I can...*, *A Conservative Philosophy* on the official Stand Up America blog cite.

Changing World Views with Sharon Hughes: http://www. changingworldviews.com/

I had the opportunity to come on Changing World Views for what would become a two show discussion on the Patriot Act. I am tremendously impressed with Sharon Hughes and her ability to deliver a quality show and to market her thoughts to the public. I believe that she may be one of the most organized radio hosts around. I'm sure this may be misconstrued by somebody somewhere, but I just totally respect, admire, and adore women who stand up in the public eye to champion conservative values. There are far too few doing this today. I'm a fan of Sharon Hughes.

The Captain's America with Matt Bruce: http:// thecaptainsamerica.blogspot.com/

Matt Bruce is a Vietnam veteran and 25-year firefighter. Bruce spends great time and effort defending and supporting the military, firefighters, and the police. I had the honor to be on the Captain's America show to talk about the Patriot Act and the show was aired in Iraq for the soldiers in the field. Outstanding! The Captain's America show is now reaching millions of listeners in 50 Countries around the World via International Broadcasting Company's "Stock Talk LIVE" broadcast and BX Radio Network's "Cool Cast" 24/7 broadcast. Go Matt Go!

Martin Dzuris Live: http://www.dzuris.com/

Martin Dzuris runs a conservative talk radio show on WRHC FM 106.7. I had the opportunity to be on his broadcast on June 18, 2007, to talk about the Patriot Act. It was a stimulating debate between Martin, his producer Nathon Lunsford, and me. Dzuris can speak about the evils of communism with absolute authority being a former citizen of the then communist controlled Czechoslovakia (now known as Czech Republic). After escaping the communists in the late 1980s and having a spiritual awakening in the United States, Dzuris is now a conservative warrior. I really enjoyed being on the radio show.

The Lynn Woolley Show: http://belogical.com/

Lynn Woolley, the self proclaimed Secretary of Logic, is a witty, fast talking Texas radio host. I came on the program as a specialist on the Patriot Act and I enjoyed the brisk hard hitting conversation we had.

Straight Shooting with Troy Laplante: http://www.troylaplante. com/

The Troy Laplante show was one of the first shows I appeared on as a published book author. It was on the Troy Laplante show I first entered into an intellectual discussion on the pros and cons of the Patriot Act. Additionally, I was introduced to the first of many "callers" which I have now learned add tremendous spice to radio programs.

The New Media Journal: http://www.blogtalkradio.com/ newmediajournal

The New Media Journal is one of the best organized internet radio shows out there. Directed by Frank Salvato, the New Media Journal brings together some of the best known specialists in the field for educated discussion on the hottest topics of the day. The New Media Journal has been able to bring together both print and radio discussion in a way that compliments each other to champion conservative values.

The Andrea Shea King Show: http://www.blogtalkradio.com/ ASKShow

Andrea hosts her two-hour radio program each Sunday night at 9:00 ET on WDBO AM 580 in Orlando FL (580wdbo.com). King has two abilities that make her an excellent radio host. First, she prepares tremendously well for her shows and she exudes a confidence that comes with a familiarity of the topics to be discussed. Secondly, and I think as important, King has a gentleness that relaxes the guests and allows for a comfortable discussion of contentious issues. I was told by King that my visit to the Andrea Shea King show to discuss the Patriot Act was one of their most popular shows she has aired. While I was given the credit, I was fully aware that it was the grace by which King hosts her show that was the catalyst to our successful radio discussion on the Patriot Act.

A Newt One Radio: http://www.blogtalkradio.com/anewtone

A Newt One Radio is a hard hitting conservative talk radio show hosted by the "Sonlit Knight," with common guest "Loki," who, among others, makes up what is coined as the

"American Truth Warriors." This show is both humorous and hard hitting with a variety of interesting guests. I was fortunate to be a guest on the show twice and I was engaged by several callers with interesting questions about the Patriot Act. I find myself tuning into the show often.

America Talks with David Zublick: http://www.blogtalkradio.com/americatalks

America Talks is a conservative talk show that champions small government and a return to traditional values. I went on the America Talk's program with a feeling of uncertainty as, from my pre-show research, I did not know if I would be entering a friendly environment. There are many conservatives who do not support the Patriot Act; however, Zublick was highly professional and an excellent host despite my feeling that he was not a Patriot Act supporter. America Talks is a very interesting conservative talk show.

Political Pistachio Radio: http://www.blogtalkradio.com/politicalpistachio

Political Pistachio Radio hosted by Douglas V. Gibbs is one of the most entertaining shows I have come across on blog talk radio. The success of the show comes from the creative scheduling of guests and the ability of the host to make his growing number of listeners feel like family. Within moments of being a guest on the show, I felt at home with Mr. & Mrs. Pistachio and the many callers of the Pistachio community who all wished to be more educated about the Patriot Act.

The War Zone: http://www.blogtalkradio.com/warzone

The War Zone with SGGT Derek "Aflack" Gray is an inspirational and dynamic radio show centered around supporting the military. Gray is a living example of patriotism, having served three active tours in Iraq with the U.S. Army. I believe it is a combination of Gray's honest enthusiasm for this country and his ability to bring forth interesting guests that makes the War Zone one of the better radio shows on blog talk radio.

Radio Sgt. Freedom: http://www.blogtalkradio.com/sgtfreedom; http://www.sgtfreedom.org/

The Sgt. Freedom Campaign is a growing set of videos containing the philosophy of one of today's hardest hitting patriots of truth talk. Sgt. Freedom has no shortage of courage when it comes to facing those who would disparage the military and this country. Through the Radio Sgt. Freedom show, listeners can now receive, via internet radio, the same entertaining and inspirational words of patriotism formerly enjoyed only on video. If you like to listen to people who are not afraid to say it like it is, and kick a little liberal tail, Radio Sgt. Freedom and the Sgt. Freedom Campaign are the places to go.

Bibliography

Armstrong, C. *Religion of Violence*. Printed by permission of author.

Babbin, J. (2007, April 20). Harry Reid, loser. *Human Events.com*. Retrieved December 23, 2007, from http://www.humanevents.com/article.php?id=20347

Burtis, J. (2006, June 2). John Murtha-first the guilty verdict, then the trial. *Canada Free Press*. Retrieved December 23, 2007, from http://www.canadafreepress.com/2006/burtis060206.htm

Dorf, M. A. (2007, March 14). The FBI's misuse of national security letters reveals the often-false dichotomy between security and privacy. *FindLaw*. Retrieved March 16, 2007, from http://writ.news.findlaw.com/dorf/20070314.html

Gorin, J. (2006, July 14). Global warbling [Electronic version]. *The Christian Science Monitor*. Retrieved July 15, 2006, from http://www.csmonitor.com/2006/0714/p20s01-ussc.htm

Gwynne, P. (1975, April 28). The cooling world. *Newsweek*. Retrieved July 16, 2006, from http://www.denisdutton.com/cooling_world.htm

Hegseth, P. (2007, September 9). MoveOn.org calls Petraeus a traitor. *The Weekly Standard*. Retrieved December 23, 2007, from http://www.weeklystandard.com/Content/Public/Articles/000/000/014/091rhesh.asp

Hitchens, C. (2004, June 21). Unfairenheit 9/11, the lies of Michael Moore. *Slate*. Retrieved June 2, 2007, from http://www.slate.com/id/2102723/

Ibbetson, P. A. (2006, January 7). Why democrats fear the Patriot Act. *American Daily*. Retrieved from http://www.americandaily.com/article/11100

Ibbetson, P. A. (2006, January 28). The Patriot Act: Searching for monsters in the closet. *American Daily.* Retrieved from http://www.americandaily.com/article/11532

Ibbetson, P. A. (2006, April 4). The politics of the playground. *News By Us.* Retrieved from http://newsbyus.com/more.php?id=A2832_0_1_0_M

Ibbetson, P. A. (2006, May 19). Border security strategies from the kitchen. *News By Us.* Retrieved from http://newsbyus.com/more.php?id=A3588_0_1_0_M

Ibbetson, P. A. (2006, May 30). Border security: The ugly side of compassion. *News By Us.* Retrieved from http://newsbyus.com/more.php?id=A3752_0_1_0_M

Ibbetson, P. A. (2006, June 3). Can global warming cut your head off? *Canada Free Press.* Retrieved from http://www.canadafreepress.com/2006/ibbetson060306.htm

Ibbetson, P. A. (2006, July 27). Behind the curtain: Revisiting global warming and the war on terror. *Canada Free Press.* Retrieved from http://www.canadafreepress.com/2006/ibbetson072706.htm

Ibbetson, P. A. (2006, August 25). Fish stories: Changing the way we talk about the war on terror. *Canada Free Press.* Retrieved from http://www.canadafreepress.com/2006/ibbetson082506.htm

Ibbetson, P. A. (2006, October 17). You see it all on the farm. *The Land of the Free.* Retrieved from http://www.thelandofthefree.net/conservativeopinion/2006/10/17/you-see-it-all-on-the-farm/

Ibbetson, P. A. (2007, January 2). The wrong side of ten. *American Daily.* Retrieved from http://www.americandaily.com/article/17032

Ibbetson, P. A. (2007, March 21). Feeding the beast. *The Land of the Free.* Retrieved from http://www.thelandofthefree.net/conservativeopinion/2007/03/23/feeding-the-beast/

Ibbetson, P. A. (2007, April 13). From the pew to the pulpit: Inside the church of global warming. *Canada Free Press*. Retrieved from http://www.canadafreepress.com/2007/ibbetson041307.htm

Ibbetson, P. A. (2007, May 18). Greensburg, Kansas: When the tornado veers left. *The Conservative Voice*. Retrieved from http://www.the-conservativevoice.com/article/25461.html

Ibbetson, P. A. (2007, June 9). Michael Moore: A criminal profile. *New Media Journal*. Retrieved from http://www.newmediajournal.us/guest/p_ibbetson/06092007.htm

Ibbetson, P. A. (2007, July 7). The Value of Anger. *Capitol Hill Coffee House*. Retrieved from http://capitolhillcoffeehouse.com/more.php?id=3559_0_1_0_M

Ibbetson, P. A. (2007, July 21). Seven Minutes of Limbaugh. *Canada Free Press*. Retrieved from http://www.canadafreepress.com/2007/ibbetson072007.htm

Ibbetson, P. A. (2007, August 13). "I can...," a conservative philosophy. *Renew America*. Retrieved from http://www.renewamerica.us/columns/ibbetson/070813

Ibbetson, P. A. (2007, October 15). Death of a messenger. *Capitol Hill Coffee House*. Retrieved from http://capitolhillcoffeehouse.com/more.php?id=4231_0_1_0_M

Ibbetson, P. A. (2008, February 12). Westboro Baptist Church: The scourge of the flatlands. *Renew America*. Retrieved from http://www.renewamerica.us/columns/ibbetson/080212

Ibbetson, P. A. (2008, June 12). The five follies of Keith Olbermann. *Capitol Hill Coffee House*. Retrieved from http://capitolhillcoffeehouse.com/more.php?id=5481_0_1_0_M

Ibbetson, P. A. (2008, June 18). From pink to red. *World Net Daily*. Retrieved from http://www.worldnetdaily.com/index.php/index.php/index.php?fa=PAGE.view&pageId=67228

Ibbetson, P. A. (2008, June 30). Perseverance: Reflections from a conversation with Duane "Dog" Chapman. *Renew America.* Retrieved from http://www.renewamerica.us/columns/ibbetson/080630

Ibbetson, P. A. (2008, September 8). Gustav, God, and Michael Moore: Validations of a criminal profile. *MichNews.com.* Retrieved from http://www.michnews.com/artman/publish/article_21172.shtml

Jordan, L. J. (2007, March 9). Gonzales, Mueller admit FBI broke law. *Breitbart.* Retrieved March 11, 2007, from http://www.breitbart. com/article.php?id=D8NP15BO0&show_article=1

Kopel, D. (2004). Fifty-nine deceits in Fahrenheit 9/11. *Dave Kopel.* Retrieved June 3, 2007, from www.davekopel.org/Terror/Fiftysix-Deceits-in-Fahrenheit-911.htm

Limbaugh, R. (2007, October 19). *Betty Casey wins smear letter at $2,100,100; Rush matches bid; MC-LEF will get a total of $4.2 M.* Retrieved December 22, 2007, from http://www.rushlimbaugh. com/home/daily/site_101907/content/01125110.guest.html

Liss, K. (2005, June 22). Durbin apologizes for Nazi, Gulag, Pol Pot remarks. *Fox News.com.* Retrieved December 23, 2007, from http:// www.foxnews.com/story/0,2933,160275,00.html

Murphy, C. (2007, July 31). The dirty secret behind Kyoto. *CNN Money.com.* Retrieved March 4, 2007, from http://money.cnn. com/2006/07/28/news/international/pluggedin_murphy. fortune/ index.htm?cnn=yes

Murray, S. (2005, June 22). Durbin apologizes for remarks on abuse [Electronic version]. *Washington Post,* p.A06. Retrieved January, 5, 2008, from http://www.washingtonpost. com/wp-dyn/content/ article/2005/06/21/AR2005062101654.html

Ponte, L., & Morano, M. (2006, July). Global warming controversy: Legitimate threat or hot air? *NewsMax,* 8, 16-30.

Rule, M. (2007, February 9). CBS's Harry Smith: 'Is Al Gore a prophet?'. *NewsBusters*. Retrieved March 4, 2007, from http://newsbusters. org/node/10726

Saunders, D. (2006, June 13). Global warming fever [Electronic version]. *San Francisco Chronicle*, p. B9. Retrieved July 16, 2006, from http://www.sfgate.com/cgi-bin/article.cgi?file=/c/a/2006/06/13/ EDGDOILMDO1.DTL&ty

Tapper, J. (2007, February 26). Al Gore's 'inconvenient truth'? -- a $30,000 utility bill. *ABC News*. Retrieved March 4, 2007, from http://abcnews.go.com/Politics/print?id=2906888

Tracinski, R. (2006, June 7). Al Gore is a brave truth teller? *Real Clear Politics*. Retrieved July 12, 2006, from http://www.realclearpolitics. com/articles/2006/06/the_truth_is_inconvenient.html

White, J. (2006, August 2). Haditha Marine sues John Murtha for defamation. *Washington Post*, A05. Retrieved December 23, 2007, from http://sweetness-light.com/archive/marine-sues-murtha-for-defamation

Will, G. (2006, June 11). Gore's warming to a candidacy? *Real Clear Politics*. Retrieved July 15, 2006, from http://www.realclearpolitics. com/articles/2006/06/gores_warming_to_a_candidacy.html

WorldNetDaily.com. (2005, December 6). Kerry: 'U.S. soldiers terrorize kids.' *World Net Daily*. Retrieved December 23, 2007, from http:// www.worldnetdaily.com/news/article.asp?ARTICLE_ID=47765

Index